DINNER THIEVES

PART 1: NEVER GET FULL

ZO ALI

ISBN: 978-0-9966252-7-2
LCCN: 2016931686

Legit Styles Publishing
16501 Shady Grove Rd, Suite# 7562
Gaithersburg, MD 20898

info@legitstylespublishing.com
legitstylespublishing.com

Part 1:
Never Get Full

Chapter 1

Jinx

"NEVER A BAD THING"

"Hi Jeremy. Damn boy, you got fine over the summer." A few of my female classmates flirted as I stood in front of my locker. It was the first day of school and the first day of my senior year. I'd spent the past eleven years gearing towards this day, but I honestly didn't feel any different.

My parents named me Jeremy Christian Vaughn seventeen years ago. I was born in Italy, but because I was a military brat, I lived in Texas, Georgia, South Carolina, Kentucky, and Virginia. For the past three and a half years Memphis had become my home. Since we moved around so much I didn't have many friends. I wasn't into sports, nor did I get all worked up about the typical high school drama, I was a hustler. Anything that made dollars made sense.

School for me was a fashion show, my place to do me, and with only a few months left, I had a lot to accomplish. My pops was a retired Major in the Army, and was highly respected across the globe. Needless to say, he wasn't exactly proud that his only son was more into rap music and shooting craps than R.O.T.C. and M-16's.

The only reason we lived in Memphis so long was because my mom wanted me to have that whole high school experience. I was thankful for that. I mean I loved Central High School. It was like one of those schools from T.V. You had your jocks, your snobs, the nerds, a few potheads, your typical in-crowds, even those gothic types. I kind of mingled with everyone, especially the females.

"Good morning, handsome," my favorite chick said as she hugged me and kissed my lips.

Dominique Ellis was hands down the prettiest chick I'd ever laid eyes on. She looked just like that pretty ass basketball player Skyler Diggins and just like Skyler, my shorty could ball.

The two of us had been together for two years, both years we'd been voted cutest couple. I kissed her soft lips.

"Two weeks is way too long to be apart." She rested her head on my chest as I held her. "Where are your partners?" she asked.

"It's only 7:10. Lucky's probably still getting dressed. Icky had to pick up Nyla. Bounce is in his truck, and Hurk is at Burger King with Xaviera," I said.

Our conversation was cut short by Murder Mook's hating ass. He and I were not the coolest. We'd fought twice because of his disrespect and both times I beat him bloody! He ran a little clique of Bloods called The Wolfpack. They had numbers, but majority of them were suckers, all bark, no bite.

"Damn Ni-Ni, that lil ass phat back there." He rubbed his hands together as he eyeballed my girl's ass. It took every ounce of self-control not to break his nose. I wanted to knock all eight of his gold teeth out, fake ass thug.

"C'mon baby, walk me to my homeroom," Dominique said as she pulled me away from Mook.

I didn't budge. "I'm chillin'," I replied.

"Jeremy. Jinx, c'mon with me," Dominique pled to no avail. Before she could get me two steps, this tough ass fool, Mook, had stepped in my face.

"You better listen to your girl. Fuck around and get your ass beat," he whispered.

I noticed two of his guys were on opposite sides of me. I also spotted two teachers observing the small altercation, so I decided to play it cool. I simply backed away and walked Dominique to homeroom.

"I'm a fuck him off first chance I get."

She laughed at my statement, telling me to ignore him and focus on her. When we got to her class, we kissed and exchanged I love you's, and then I made my way down the hallway to my own homeroom.

"JV... what up my boy?" my favorite partner, Lucky, yelled my nickname so loudly that I stopped and turned around.

The two of us gave each other dap. "Boy that's a cold ass Jordan's set," I said.

"My sister got it in Miami. You know money green is my muhfuckin' color. I got a white one too."

He flirted with a couple females while we chit chatted. Lucky was a true player. The two of us had been cool since the 9th grade and he hadn't changed. All he cared about were girls, clothes, and money.

He asked if any of our other partners had made it yet. I told him I hadn't seen them and then we both spotted Ebony Young as she and her best friend walked by. "Brah, please tell me you hit that this summer. Y'all worked at the pool three months together," he said.

"I didn't try to. I fuck with Gangster," I said referring to Ebony's boyfriend.

He laughed. "Fuck that fat albino lookin' fool. Anyway, what we doing after school?" he asked.

"We'll figure it out. I'm going to class." I gave him dap and then headed my way while he went his.

Lucky

"LUCKY'S CHARM"

I sat in the rear of the class and pretended to listen to my math teacher. My eyes were roaming all over the room, observing all the females. Majority of them I'd already had, but there were two whom I'd yet to get that had my attention at the present time.

Girls were like a drug for me. In fact, they gave me the best high. My mother always said it was in my blood to be a ladies' man. My dad was a trick and my mom was his favorite prostitute. She was smart though, she never worked for a pimp and when she got pregnant she convinced my old man to marry her. He died two weeks after my birth, a victim of a botched robbery attempt.

My mom had a set of twins before I was born; my 21-year-old sisters, Maria and Victoria, and she herself was a twin. I was raised in a home with four females, each just as beautiful as the rest so naturally being a chick magnet was easy for me.

My looks were always the gifts I was cursed with. My dad was Black, but my mom is a mixture of Puerto Rican, Black, and White, so just like my sisters I was bi-racial. Growing up, the trouble I got into was either because I was with someone else's girl or I had to defend one of the women in my family. In my 18 years, I'd earned every ounce of my street credibility. Lorenzo "Lucky" Mendes was no punk and the trillest of the trill knew it best.

The bell rang, signaling the end of the school day. I hurried out to my car, the one I'd spent all summer working on, and tossed my book bag in the trunk. While I waited on Jinx, I sat on the hood of my Chevy Malibu. The car sat on 26" chrome rims and the paint flipped from blue, to purple, to green.

"Hi Lorenzo," Smurf said, she was one of the cheerleaders, a petite little redbone, one of the few seniors I hadn't slept with.

I looked her over and smiled approvingly. "You look good in that dress. You must have known green is my favorite color."

She smiled and replied. "Is that right? Well, which one of these females is your fav?"

"See, that's why I like you, you get straight to the point. It doesn't matter who my favorite is, just know I think you're the baddest."

She sat next to me. "Anyone ever tell you you look like Drake with these thick eyebrows?"

I laughed at her remark. "N'all, but my mom thinks I'm handsome," I said with a cocky smirk. "There's your sidekick," I pointed towards Smurf's bff, Birdie.

"What you say about me?" she asked.

"Over here running game," Smurf added.

I smiled at them both. "I was just tellin' her how you might be the baddest female in school."

"I thought I was?" Smurf added.

"You too... Anyway, what y'all bout to get into?" I checked my watch. "I'm headed to the crib if y'all wanna kick it."

Before they could reply, my boy, Icky, pulled up in his mom's Yukon. I let him know I was chilling with Smurf and Birdie. The females got in Birdie's Honda and let me know they'd meet me at my house.

"Both of 'um?" Icky asked once they'd pulled off. "You lucky fucker. Get one in for me too my boy..."

I gave him dap, got in my ride, and pulled off. He was right. I was what my name suggested, Lucky.

Chapter 2
Icky
"SLICK ICKY"

For as long as I can remember, I wanted to be famous. I wanted to be someone of importance, not just another face in the crowd. I mean, my dad was a legend in the streets of Memphis, as were my uncles and my brother. I could clearly recall the looks of terror I'd get at the mere mention of their names. The way people reacted made me wish I was just like them. I was a fiend for fame, willing to obtain it by any means.

17 years ago, I was born and named Ike Turner. My dad was a big-time drug dealer and my mom was his main chick. During my childhood, my parents were in and out of prison. My uncles raised me, the streets raised them, and naturally, those values and principles were embedded in me. When I was six years old, my parents went to federal prison. My dad got thirty years, my mom got eight. By age 10, I was hustling. I started as a lookout, but six months later, I was pushing rocks for my Uncle Boney.

I was in the sixth grade when I caught my first charge, that's when I met my best friend Hurk. The two of us went to an alternative school. It was there that our reputations spread. The following year, we took over our junior high. When people didn't give us the respect we demanded, we took it.

I was raised in the heart of South Memphis, on Greenwood Street. I learned to keep my hands clean in the hood, never shitting where I lay.

I was standing on the curb talking on the phone when my uncle pulled up in his red drop-top Jag. He had his man, Diego, with him. Boney was hood rich, mostly from moving bricks of coke and pounds of weed. He'd spoiled the hell out of me, but he never condoned me hustling. Every now and then he'd tossed me a little work, but ninety percent of the time it was out of the question. He didn't want me to be like him or my pops, and though I respected that, I wasn't listening.

"Damn, Unc, let me test drive that Jag," I said.

He got out and gave me dap. "Not today. Where's Cool?" Boney asked.

"She went to the mall with her boyfriend," I replied as I greeted Diego. I tossed my uncle the money my mom left for him to put on my dad and brother's books. "You going to see Killer this weekend?"

"Yeah, I'm going to see your brother too." I let him know I wanted to go. "I need something from you."

He looked at Diego then me. "I heard you been fuckin' with Gangster Greg from Riverside. You payin' bout a stack an ounce." He shook his head, obviously disappointed in me. "Diego, give him four and a half ounces. Icky, I want $3000, that's enough for you to get your own. And don't ask me for no more dope..." He got in his car.

"I'll see you Friday, Unc," I snatched the paper bag from Diego and ran in the house.

I put the work in my closet, took a quick shower, and went to get my girl, Nyla, from the beauty shop. And though I kept a lot of groupies, one chick had my heart.

Nyla Crump and I had been together for three years. We met at a Yo Gotti concert. She was with a few of her friends when she approached me out the blue. I'll never forget that day. I wore a fresh purple and blue Coogi set, with blue suede Jordan's. She told me that I looked like her favorite rapper Young Jeezy. I smiled, showing all sixteen of my rose gold teeth and told her she was prettier than Meagan Good. We exchanged numbers and went out twice in a week. After the third date, she gave me her virginity and I gave her my heart.

My phone rang while I was in the parking lot waiting on her. It was my partner, Bounce, calling to let me know about the shootout in the projects. He said the Wolfpack had gotten into a fight with the Claiborne Home Crips and it went down.

I hung up when Nyla got in the car. I complimented her honey colored

Marilyn Monroe style, and asked if she was hungry.

"I made Jinx buy me a ten-piece hot wing dinner. He brought Hurk's sisters up here. Angel has a crush on him. Anyway, I told my momma about the baby and my sister has already started shopping."

"I told Cool. She wants us to move in together...I think it's a good idea."

She smiled. "You'll have to tell my momma."

"Alright." I kissed her lips, thinking to myself that I had to get my shit in order. No child of mine would ever want for anything, nor would my girl.

Bounce

"BOUNCE BACK"

Life has a funny way of changing people. Whether it's for the better or for worse, life can be just as unpredictable as the weather. For the first 13 years of my life, I had the fairytale existence. My dad was an executive at FedEx making over a hundred and eighty grand a year. My mom was the state's top criminal defense attorney and partner at a prestigious firm. The world was in the palm of my hands. I never wanted for anything. Then suddenly it all changed for the worse.

My parents were murdered by a man my mom used to work for. Since then, I've been living with my older sister who followed my mom's footsteps and became a lawyer herself. After the death of my parents, I kept my guards up. I mean, other than my sister and my three-year-old nephew, the only people I gave a damn about were my four partners. Had it not been for them, I probably would not have turned out as normal as I am.

I'd always been quick tempered, but over the past four years it had become even shorter. The smallest things set me off. My sister said it was because I hid my emotions, but I blame it on my low tolerance for bullshit. I'd been involved in more fights than Floyd Mayweather.

"Aye Bounce, what's up with you and Star Cooper?" Lucky tossed me a cigar and a bag of weed. He was the player of the group. Lil brah had a chick at every high school in the city.

I crumbled weed onto some newspaper. "She playing games. Hurk said she fucked with Youngblood."

"Youngblood? That rap shit got him on major league girls now," Jinx added. He was texting on his phone, not really into the conversation. "He bought a blood red Escalade; Iysis was over Stacy's house in that mu'fucker."

I looked at Lucky. "You hate that?" I asked.

He popped the collar on his polo shirt and said, "Fuck shawty, I got more bitches than playboy magazine! I fucked Smurf and Birdie yesterday. Plus, I got Kourtney and GG. You want me to keep going?"

"Fuck all that, what's up with your sister?" Hurk asked. He was the quiet one, but his bite was lethal. Out of all five of us, Hurk was the most liked and respected. He didn't tolerate any bullshit from anyone, especially not us. He was the big brother.

"My sister will run circles around you," Lucky replied.

My phone rang. It was my home girl Valencia. She wanted me to pick her up from work. Of course I agreed so I grabbed my keys before I was even off the phone.

"Where are you going?" Hurk asked.

"Gotta pick up Val from work. What y'all about to do?" I asked.

Lucky and Jinx got their stuff and headed to the door. "I'm on my way to the crib," Hurk said.

The three of them walked out before me. I locked the front door and asked Lucky where he was headed. He let me know he and Jinx were going to the mall. Jinx reminded me that we were all meeting at IHOP at 6:30 the next morning.

I started my gold Cutlass. Yo Gotti's *Racks* came pumping through the system in my trunk. I pulled off right after the three of them left. Fifteen minutes later, I was parking in front of the Old Navy on Poplar and Highland.

I watched Valencia as she and her manager talked near the front door. Valencia Yale was a majorette at Central High School. The two of us dated in the 10th and 11th grade. She was a ghetto princess, the type the thugs adored and the females respected even more. Monica was her idol, and at first glance, you'd know it. Her hair, style, face, and body all reminded people of the R&B singer.

"You drive." I got out and walked to the other side of the car. "Why you getting off so early?"

She adjusted the seat and changed my music. "I had to come in for a couple of hours. My brother went to the studio so he couldn't pick me up anyway. I don't want you to get in trouble because I heard you fuck with Star Cooper now."

"Whatever. You going to the game Friday night?" I lit a blunt and cracked my window.

"Yes. You heard about the party at The Honeycomb?"

"Jinx mentioned it. Your booh is performing."

She snatched the blunt. "Don't nobody like Yellow Boy's pale ass, with that unibrow. Anyway, you're taking me to the party. Matter of fact, you're taking me to the game too."

"What about Terio?" I asked her.

She smiled. "Everybody knows I'm yours...gimme a kiss you're too much," she said.

I kissed her lips and replied. "But you handle me very well… Your big head ass…"

Hurk

"HURK-N-JERK"

"Hey big brother." My three-year-old sister, Amy, met me as soon as I walked through the front door.

I picked her up and kissed her golden-brown cheeks. Amy was the youngest, but I was the eldest and the only boy out of my mom's five kids. After me were my 16-year-old twin sisters, Angelina and Alicia, and my 14-year-old sister, Alexis.

I've never met my dad, but the streets knew him well. His name was Anthony Hunter Sr., and everyone said I was just like him. I didn't embrace it simply for the fact that he left my mom before I was even born. Often working two full-time jobs, my moms slaved to keep us happy, keep food in the house, and pay bills.

I wasn't a lazy cat. Since I was ten, I had a job or a hustle. Physically, I was always a lot bigger than the cats my age. However, at 6'5" and 240 pounds, I wasn't into sports because getting money was my sport. My family was my motivation.

"Where is Alexis?" I asked Amy.

"In her room on the phone with her boyfriend." She pulled me down the hallway towards the room Alexis and the twins slept in.

"Hey big brother," Alicia said. She was in the bathroom perming her hair.

Alicia was the younger twin, but unlike Angel, she was focused on her future. Angel was the boy crazy one.

"What y'all eat?" I asked Alicia.

She laughed as Angel walked out of the bedroom. My booh bought us pizza. He got you one too. Momma said to call her." Angel kissed my cheek then helped Alicia put the rest of the perm in.

"Alexis you on my phone?" I asked her. She was in my bed with the lights out.

"I'll be off before 9. I promise."

"Brother, Jinx is on the phone." Angel gave me the other phone.

"What up, lil brah?" I answered.

"Aye, you get that pizza that I bought?" I looked at Angel while Jinx talked. "Your crazy ass sister called me. Anyway, I'm on my way back over there, I want you to see something."

I gave Angel the phone. "I thought your booh bought y'all dinner?"

"Boy please, you know I love Jeremy Vaughn. I'm having his kids one day. He got a new car, a green and gold Cutlass on 26's and he let me and Amy ride to Pizza Hut with him earlier. Anyway, go shower, you smell like burgers and onion rings," Angel said.

Amy ran out of the other bathroom with water all over her hands and feet. "I turned the shower on for you."

I laughed as she ran into my mom's room. I loved my sisters and I was determined to give them the world or die trying.

Chapter 3

Lucky

"A LUCKY DAY"

Three days later

"I'm at *Toya's* but I'm almost done eating."

"Well, I'm about to leave. Make sure you pick up your money from Debbie. I love you."

"I love you too Sugar Momma. Have fun in New York." I hung up my phone and finished the last of my macaroni and chicken fried steak. I was inside my favorite soul food joint named *Toya's,* having my usual Friday meal.

The place was named after its beautiful owner and had been open for the past five years. Sugar Momma knew the owner; it was she who introduced me to the place. I loved the food, but I enjoyed Toya Davis even more. She was married to a cat named Buck Davis who was a street legend. I never met him, but he and Sugar Momma ran in the same circle. For the last ten years, he'd been in federal prison, but despite that fact, his beautiful wife still held him down.

"You alright, Lucky?" Toya asked. She was fine and sexy like a video model.

I wiped my hands and mouth. "I'm cool. You look cute today. I like that skirt," I complimented her, to which she thanked me. She then asked if I was going to the big football game between Hamilton and Central. I told her I was and then I asked about the photos she added to her wall.

"Those are my kids," she answered proudly. "The two little girls in the front are Alicia and Bria. Bria is my mini me. Alicia's mom is Mac Goo's sister. The light-skinned girl with the curly hair is Princess. The boy with the braids is my son Toby...the other boy is Buck Jr. and the diva with the gray eyes is Miss August. My husband wants another boy," she added.

"He's been gone ten years. He's only 33, I'm 31. He got locked up the day after our wedding and hasn't been home since."

"Damn, you waited the whole time?" I asked.

She laughed. "Of course I have. Part of the game is learning to accept the bad side too. My man comes home in three days. You should come by Monday. I'll introduce you to him," she said before she walked away.

I watched her ass bounce until she was out of sight, then I left my waitress a tip and left. It was 4:30 when I got in my car. I had some time to kill before I went to the game, so I went to get the money my Aunt Debbie had for me.

She was washing her Lexus coupe when I pulled up. Aunt Debbie had on daisy dukes and a wife beater, looking like Ms. Parker from the movie Friday. She loved the attention, obvious by the fact that she had five young guys stalking her from the porch next door.

"Hey, my Lucky baby." She kissed my cheek as she gave me the cash from her bra. "That's $1500. You hungry?" she asked.

"I just left Toya's." I kissed her cheek. "I have to go meet Jinx."

"Is he 18 yet? I can't wait to give his cute self some pussy. I tried to tell Vicky he likes her."

I got in my car and told auntie I'll call her in a day or two. On my way to the mall, I called Jinx. He told me to pick him up from his house. When I got there, he was in the driveway. As soon as I parked, he got in the car.

"You just missed Tia and Staci. Tia asked about you," Jinx said. "Staci wants me to take her to the movies after the game. I need to borrow $2500, my Mexican g'on let me get a 9 piece for $5000. I'll get your money back in a couple of days," he said.

He passed me a picture of his dream house.

"In three years, I plan to buy that house. College ain't g'on pay for it," he said.

I shook my head and smiled. "I'm wit'cha then. Whatever you need, I gotcha," I replied.

Hurk

"THE MAN-CHILD"

"C'mere," Pasha Lewis called my name as my guys and I stood near the concession stand.

Pasha was a senior like us, but she was so far ahead of the other chicks I knew. She was a dancer and everything from her weave to the Red Bottoms she wore screamed top-notch.

It was halftime, the score was tied at 17 and the stadium was so packed that the vendors ran out of tickets.

I made my way to her. "What's up?" I asked.

She played with her hair as she asked where my girl was. She let me know she wasn't trying to be disrespectful to Xaviera, although she was feeling me. I made sure I flirted with her, complimenting everything from her flawless hair and her makeup, to the way her low rise jeans hugged her 38 inch hips.

Lucky walked over and squeezed a handful of Pasha's ass. "Shit girl, you're too young to have all that ass!"

She pushed him. "That's why don't nobody like your disrespectful ass!"

He laughed at her comment. "I got more hoes then King magazine. Matter of fact, where Cookie with her cat eyed mouse lookin' ass?" Lucky asked.

"Anyway, are you coming to the club tonight?" Pasha asked me. I told her yes, but my attention was focused on my girl and her friends as they made their way towards us.

I asked Lucky to run interference, which he quickly did. He started flirting with Pasha, trying to cop another feel of her donkey booty.

"C'mon and buy me a sour pickle. Fuck around and make me hurt you and her," Xaviera whispered as Pasha switched her hips and walked away.

"Cut that shit out. All that kissing and cuddling looking like 50 Cent and Kelly Rowland." Lucky dodged Xaviera's punches, still laughing and teasing us all the while. "Hurk, I'm out. I have a date." He gave me dap then made his way out of the stadium.

I walked hand-in-hand with my girl to the concession stand. The two of us continued to cuddle and flirt while we waited in line. Xaviera and I had been a couple since the seventh grade, never breaking up. No matter the temptation, I remained one hundred percent faithful. I reminded her of that when she mentioned Pasha's attraction to me.

"You know Nyla caught Icky snorting cocaine." She put my fitted hat on her head. "She claims they broke up," she told me.

"They'll be back together by Monday morning," I laughed.

A crowd had formed near where I had left Jinx and Icky. I couldn't see exactly what was going on, but when I saw Murder Mook I knew things were about to get crazy. Xaviera called my name, but I kept moving towards the crowd, and moving a few people as well.

"Do something then my nigga." Murder Mook tried to step to Jinx, but I stopped him.

"Chill out Mookie," I said. He looked me up and down, laughing as he asked if Jinx was my bitch. "This ain't what you want," I said.

Dominique pulled Jinx away from Mook. "Watch out, I'm tryna see what he wanna do. He must be strapped, cause he know I'll beat the piss out of his bladder. Bitch ass nigga g'on fuck up and get his nose broken again." Jinx was mad now.

Mook's dumb ass failed to heed the warning. As soon as he moved like he was trying to attack, Jinx punched him until he fell face first onto the pavement. That's all it took for the rumble to jump off. The entire Wolfpack jumped in!

Icky, Bounce, Jinx, and I handled the seven of them with ease. They didn't have a chance.

Bock! Bock! Bock!

Three gunshots cleared the chaotic scene.

I grabbed my girl and rushed to my car. I knew it wasn't over, Murder Mook would try us again, and we'd be more than ready for whatever he and his guys wanted to do

Chapter 4
Icky
"ALL IN THE NAME"

Two weeks later

I rolled over and checked my alarm clock. It was 6:15 in the morning. I was officially eighteen and I was ready to start my day. The day before, my Uncle Boney bought me a white on white Crown Victoria. He let me know that Killer D had a gift for me too, which had me more excited than a kid at Christmas.

I was just getting out of the shower, putting on a fresh pair of ash gray jeans when my mom walked in. She hugged me and then gave me the gift she and her boyfriend got for me. I put the iced-out diamond chain around my neck and admired myself as I stood in the mirror.

"Here, Killer D told me to give you this." She tossed a backpack at my feet. While she waited for me to open it she tied her dreads into a knot. Cool wasn't your typical mom she was only thirteen years older than I was. I never called her mom and she never hid her lifestyle. She lived fast, loved dope boys, and was still affiliated with the *Gutter Tribe.*

I passed her the blunt I'd lit. "Big shout out to the Homey Slick Icky... that's from OG Killer and the Big Homey Dirty D-Gutter Tribe . What up, Cool?" The DJ on the radio gave me a shout out.

"That's a survival kit. Killer D said make him proud," Cool said.

I opened the backpack. Inside was a glock 40, a kilo of coke, and $20,000. "If you fuck around and go to jail make sure it's worth it. Your daddy and your brother had a good run, but you see where they ended up… And since you're 18, you have to pay some bills or move out… That's what Killer D said," Cool continued. "You and Nyla should get a place."

I laced up my shoes. "She wants to wait until we graduate. I'll be home late tonight." I put the cash in my pocket and the gun on my hip. "I love you."

I ran out to my car and smashed off. I had to pick up Nyla and drop her off at school.

When I got to her house, she was standing on the porch looking excited to see me. She met me with open arms and a big kiss when I got out of the car. She still wasn't ready for school so she led me up to the house and to her room. "I want to stop and get something to eat," she said.

"I want to eat you," I replied. I pinned her on her back and kissed the tattoo of my name on her left breast. "I want some," I whispered.

She smiled as she took off her shirt. "Let's do it then," she said.

Jinx

"JUMP BACK JINX"

"May I speak to Jeremy?"

I tossed Lucky the dice and walked from the carport out to the front of the driveway. "What's up Miss Staci Armstrong?"

"Nothing. I'm just trying to come see you. Are you home?"

"N'all, I'm at Lucky's."

She whispered to someone. "Okay, me and GG are at the Wendy's on Elvis Presley Blvd. Do you want anything?"

"A frosty. I'm in the front so come on," I told her.

Lucky joined me when I sat on the trunk of his Malibu. I let him know Staci and GG were on their way. While we chit-chatted, Gangster Greg and the homey Shotgun walked from the carport.

"Here, we bout to roll. Y'all stay outta trouble," Shotgun said as he gave me the dice. He was a couple years older than us, but we were tight with his sister Jackie. Gangster Greg was the homey from South Memphis. He's the one that shot up the game the night we got into the fight with the Wolfpack.

"Sell me a hundred pack of kush," he said.

"This is on me my guy. Y'all gangsters be safe." I tossed him the rest of the half ounce we'd been smoking and then showed them love before they left.

As they pulled off, Staci's mustard colored Mustang turned the corner. Staci was the baddest chick I knew. The girl had skin the color of cocoa butter, silky black hair that was always shiny and well kept, the sexiest green eyes, and the swag and style of a young Beyoncé. People couldn't tell whether she was black or white, but they knew she was fine.

She got out wearing a fitted sweat suit and matching blue and white stiletto heels.

"You make me want to leave the one I'm with, start a new relationship with you," I said, trying my best to impersonate Usher.

She blushed and stood back on her legs. "Here's your damn frosty, silly self."

Lucky spoke to Staci and walked out to talk to GG. GG and Staci were god sisters. Her and Lucky had a thing going on although they didn't take it seriously.

"You look cute today I love the educated thug look," Staci said while joining me on the trunk of the car. "Anyway, where is your booh?" She nibbled on her chicken nuggets.

I couldn't help but notice the way she rolled her eyes. "I think she's with her friends," I said.

"She must not know you're with your sidekick," she replied. We laughed at Lucky as he fed GG french fries. "Tell your friend don't hurt my girl."

"Let them do them, ain't nobody in your business because you like dread heads."

She snatched my frosty and drank some. You're just mad because your girl ain't me," she added.

A silver Galant pulled up. "Aye Jinx, you good?" the driver asked. I walked out to the car and served him two $50 packs of cocaine. I put the money in Staci's waistline when I returned to her. She complained about me serving out in the open but I wasn't listening.

"Real talk, how long are we gonna play games?" I asked as I put my arms around her waist. She mentioned something about not wanting to be my number two or three. Before I answered, Lucky and GG told us they were headed to the mall.

I sat on Staci's car while she stood in between my legs. She rested her back on my chest as we watched the sunset in silence.

"Stop," she moaned as I softly kissed her neck, just behind her left ear.

I slid my hands inside her sweatpants and rested them just above the silky hair between her legs. I wasn't sure if she meant for me to stop, so I just waited.

"Can I have a kiss?" she asked.

She moved her hair to the left side of her face and then looked over her shoulder at me. Her breathing was faster, like she was nervous. She let me slip my tongue into her mouth and moaned when my finger found her tight slit.

“Jeremy that hurts,” she moaned when I slid a finger into her pussy. She opened her legs a little more and reached back to grip my hardness while I played with her virgin vagina. She bit my bottom lip when she came.

We were so caught up that neither one of us noticed Sugar Momma until she slammed her car door.

“Your mannish ass,” she said to me. “Where's Lucky?” She hugged me and Staci, still smiling when I told her Lucky took GG to the mall.

“Give me some money,” she demanded. I gave her some money.

“Tell Lucky I'll pick my car in the morning.”

I pulled Staci to her car.

“I need to change my panties,” she blushed. “Jinx don't make me regret being with you.”

I kissed her lips. “Just roll with me shawty, I promise it'll be worth it,” I assured her, meaning every word.

Chapter 5
Bounce
"TEMPER, TEMPER"

"You've only been home for three days, don't get into any trouble."

I sat at the kitchen table and fixed myself a plate. My sister kissed my cheek then continued her conversation while my nephew bragged about going to the zoo.

"Boy please, I'm taking my son to the zoo today." She kissed Zion's cheek. "You think your wife will be okay with that? Okay I'll see you there." She hung up, but had a blank stare on her face.

"You cool?" I asked after a few minutes.

She joined us at the table with a schoolgirl smile on her face. "That was an old friend, my favorite client."

"He must be really special. You have love in your eyes," I said.

"Shut up and stop eating so fast," she said. She kissed Zion and told him to go brush his teeth. "So are you and Val back together?"

I rinsed my plate. "Only friends, but we've talked about it going further."

The house vibrated from the loud music outside. It was Young Jeezy's *Crazy World*, Icky's favorite song.

"You need to check your crazy ass friend!" my sister snapped.

"I will. I love you, have a good day, and take pictures."

I grabbed my backpack and hurried out to Icky's car.

"Turn that shit down, this is a white neighborhood." He laughed as he passed me the blunt.

"My fault. Your sister must be tripping."

"You already know." I tasted the weed. "Damn boy! You got good kush. Who got this? Jinx?"

He smiled. "I got it from a lick I hit last night. You must didn't see them 26's on my car." He switched the song to another Jeezy classic.

"Boney bought this car and the rims, you ain't robbed shit. You need to stop listening to all that Gucci Mane." He reached underneath his seat and pulled out a pistol.

"Me and Hurk been on one... You think Burger King got that Maxima on 24's?" I passed the blunt.

"What y'all get?"

"$2600 each, a couple pounds of dro, these rims, and a Jacobs watch Hurk kept." He pulled his black hoodie over his head. "I'm like John Wayne out here. I done shot two mu'fuckers already this week..."

"You crazy," I said, still shocked about what I just found out from my best friend.

"Crazy? You ain't seen shit yet. I'm trying to buy Nyla a car for Christmas." He turned into the school lot and let me out. "I'm going to drop my baby off at school. I'll be back around lunch time."

I made my way into the building. Before I was in the door good, I was stopped by Star Cooper. Star was Gangsta Greg's little sister, and as sexy as she was, that's why no one would mess with her. Shawty was fine, but her brother was crazier than 4 Fool. Who'd date a chick with a 21-year-old 6'3", 250 pound, short tempered, gunslinger for a brother?

"What's up shawty? You in full *Pink Friday* mode ain't you?"

She kissed my cheek and wrapped my arm around her waist as we made our way down the hallway.

"Damn Star, how you get in these jeans?" I asked.

She put my hand in the back pocket of her pink Guess jeans. "You should see me with um off," she replied.

I whispered, "I wanna fuck."

She smiled and left me standing at my locker with a semi hard on.

"Damn I wonder if she still cry when she nuts," Lucky said as soon as he made it to the locker. Before I could answer, Murder Mook intentionally bumped into me.

“C'mere, bitch.” I scooped him up and slammed him on the floor. I busted him open with a three-punch combination to the face.

“I told you boy,” I taunted him as Coach Tate pulled me off him. Lucky stomped Murder Mook until Coach Hill grabbed him. By that time, Mook was out cold and bleeding all over the floor.

Jinx

"3 FOR ONE"

"That fool damn near broke his back. I tried to stomp his heart out." Lucky continued to tell us about their fight with Murder Mook. The whole beef with the Wolfpack was getting bigger than we anticipated. I knew it was about to get uglier, but no one seemed to care too much.

"I hate I missed it. Anyway, what y'all about to get into?"

I checked the text I just received from my connect.

"I'm meeting I-40 and Vago," I added. Lucky and Bounce had dates, Icky was at Nyla's, and to my surprise, Hurk said he was rolling with me.

The two of us got into my Cutlass and left Lucky's. The first stop was to drop off some hot wings to Hurk's sisters.

"Hey Jinx, hey big brother," Amy met us as soon as we stepped inside. I gave her a kiss and then made my way to Angel's room.

"What's up Lexis? Hey Alicia, where's your crazy ass twin?"

Angel pushed me out of the doorway. She was just getting out of the shower, only wearing a towel wrapped around her body. I had to catch myself from staring because shawty looked good.

"Thank you Jinx." Alicia got the food and headed to the kitchen.

Angel glanced at me and smiled. "How long are you going to stare at me?"

I laughed. "You aren't on my level but you look good though."

My phone vibrated. "I'm on my way," I told Vago. "Aye Hurk I got to make a run.

"Go ahead. I'm going over Pasha's house. You got some green on you?" He was laying clothes out and running shower water.

"It's in the car. Angel Monique, come get this for big brah!" I hurried out to the car.

Angel came outside. She walked up on me, close enough for her breast to touch my body. "I turn 16 next week and you're taking me to the movies. I need to get my hair and nails

done and you need to take me to the mall so we can get Alicia a gift too."

"Take your little hot ass in the house," I told her.

She looked me over and licked her lips. "I can't wait until you're mine. Be safe baby, I'll call you before I go to sleep."

I watched her walk away. Her little ass looked good in those sweatpants. I got in the car once and she was in the house.

Thirty minutes later, I was parking behind the steel plant where I usually met Vago and I-40. I called twice but they didn't answer.

"What the fuck!" I noticed something strange. I-40 and Vago had their hands up. Two guys had them at gunpoint. From my car, they couldn't see me, but I had a bird's eye view of the robbery.

I have to do something. I got my .38 revolver from my console, got out of the car, and I crept through the darkness until I was in earshot.

"Please, you can have the drugs, just let us live," Vago pleaded with the gunman.

"Shut up," the gunmen replied. He told the other gunmen to take Vago's car keys and load the drugs into their car.

Pop! Pop! Pop! Pop! Pop!

I shot them both. I didn't see a reason to waste time. I figured this was my way of getting in good with my Mexican partners.

"It's me," I said as I stepped out where they could see me. I-40 picked up one of the guns and emptied it into the prone bodies of the two men who seconds ago had him at gunpoint.

"Thank you," he said. I asked him what happened. "That's not important, just know that you will be properly rewarded. You are forever in good graces. Vago, give him all the cocaine and let's get out of here." He shook my hand. "I'll call you soon my friend, this shipment is on me."

I took the two duffel bags and hurried to my car. I got out of there as quickly as I could, driving straight to Icky's.

I parked, but I didn't get out. "Oh shit, I'm on now," I shouted once I opened the bags. *6...7...8...9...10 free bricks and 50 pounds of Cali Bud. Shit yeah, I'm about to shut the city down. Can't tell nobody about this shit though, real gangsters move in silence, just like I did when I merked them fools.* I laughed at the thought. My years of military school had actually come in handy, now it was time for my hustler's ambition to takeover. I was 17 and had literally walked into a six-figure situation. I had no excuses not to go to the next level, and I wouldn't stop until I did.

Chapter 6
Jinx
"THE COME UP"

"What's up booh. You busy?"

I stepped off the porch so I could hear the voice on the other line. "You asked me the same thing when you called an hour ago."

"And when I call in another hour I'll ask again," Angel's jazzy ass replied. "Anyway, have you had anything to eat?" I told her no. She said, "That's a shame… See, that's exactly why I check on you all the time. I'm bringing you a plate."

"A'ight bye."

I hung up at the same time that Pasha and Cookie pulled up. Pasha had called earlier and said she needed four and a half ounces of coke. It had only been a day and a half since my big come up, but I was already getting rid of my product like new Jordan's on Saturday. My strategy was simple; I sold a better product at a better price.

"Damn boy, you're so damn cute, you'd better be glad Dominique is my girl," Cookie said.

"That shit sounds good… Anyway just give me $3200 for this." I handed the brown paper sack to Pasha. "I might stop by the club tonight, see if y'all still talking that shit about Nikki." I counted the money she gave me, adding it to the knot I already had.

Pasha smiled after kissing my cheek. "Whenever you get ready, I'm ready." She and Cookie walked to her Acura and left.

For the next 30 minutes or so, I continued to do my thing. I sold everything. If someone had three dollars and wanted to get a joint of weed, I sold it. Plus, I had so much free cocaine I was simply using it to build clientele for the future. I was on a mission- *never get full.* When Angel and Alexis pulled up and Hurk's Maxima, I was standing in the driveway with Icky and my partner, Lil Mane.

"Hey y'all. Hey baby," Angel spoke to my guys and then hugged me after handing me my food. I lifted the top off of the tupperware bowl.

"Who made this?"

"I did. It's fried catfish and spaghetti."

"My momma told me don't eat anybody's spaghetti."

She rolled her eyes. "Boy please you'll eat whatever I feed you... Now walk me to the car so I can go."

I couldn't help but smile at how good she looked in her jeans. Angel was starting to have an affect on me. I spoke to Alexis, then asked Angel where they were headed. She told me that they were going to the mall, then to the movies. She also reminded me that her and Alicia turned 16 in three days and she was expecting me to take her out.

"Here, get Alicia something from me and don't call me all damn night." I gave her a couple hundred dollars more than what she needed. She smiled knowingly.

"I'll call you if I want to. Anyway, go eat, and be careful out here." She pulled off.

"Aye... Jinx, you fuckin' Lil Angel?" Icky asked.

"N'all." I walked into the house and put my food in the microwave. Lil Mane asked about Alexis, so I told him who she was. Once my food was done, I sat at the table and started to eat. Icky was busy over the stove cooking an ounce of coke into crack.

"Aye... Jinx what that *D.T.G.* on your hand mean?" Lil Mane checked out the fresh tattoo on my left hand.

"*Dinner Thief Gangsta.*"

He looked at me, then at Icky. "That's the name of your gang?"

"Yup... You tryna get put down?" I wiped my mouth and hands.

"What did I have to do?" he asked.

"Get jumped in as soon as brah is done eating. Don't tell Pasha and Cookie though, you know they still treat you like a baby," Icky added.

I laughed. "I'll put them down too. Anyway, let's do it now, then I'll take you to get your tattoo," I said. Icky finished what he was doing, and then followed me and Lil Mane outside.

Fop! Fop! Fop!

Before we even made it off the porch, I punched him three times. "You better fight back."

He smiled after punching both me and Icky. It was official now, I was putting my first seed down and before long I'd have a thousand more just as gutter as he would be.

Chapter 7
Jinx
"JEWELS"

One month later

"Hello," I answered.

"Hey, are you still mad at me."

"Mad for what? I mean, you made your choice. I don't have to like it, but I have to respect it."

She let out a sigh of frustration. "Whatever Jeremy. I have a plane to catch, I guess I'll talk to you when I get back."

I put my phone in my console after Dominique hung up on me.

Angel looked over at me and laughed. "Who was that, Staci or Dominique?" When I failed to respond, she rolled her eyes and asked again.

"None of your business." I turned my David Ruffin up and tried to tune Angel out, but she wouldn't let me. She turned the music down and looked at me.

"If it was Staci, I think you're playing with fire. That girl is too materialistic for you. Plus, she's sprung on Ziggy."

I lit a blunt and cracked the sunroof. "You think so?"

"Yes. They've been together for years. Plus, he spoils her. If it was Dominique, I'm glad you broke up. I hope they both break your heart."

"It's like that? I figured you were a hater," I said as I turned my stereo back up.

She pulled the visor down and put on her makeup. "You act like I'm supposed to be cool with them. That's my competition."

"I'm too far out of your league, you still have the days of the week on your lil panties."

"You're only a year older than I am. You didn't go to kindergarten, otherwise you'd be a junior instead of a senior and as far as my panties go, I only wear thongs or boy shorts." She turned her lip up and rolled her eyes at me. "Just for that, when I let you burst my cherry; I'm biting you and scratching your punk ass."

I laughed so hard I choked on the weed smoke. "You're too wild."

"Hmp, I'm dead serious. You know I'm crazy about you... You have crazy ass swag, with your sexy brown self..." She played with my ear. "I'm almost ready too."

I couldn't help but blush, but I was glad I was pulling up to Macy's.

"Get out, go to work, and don't call me every hour on the hour."

"Quit acting like you don't love the attention." She got her purse and then kissed the corner of my mouth. "I don't want to get you in no trouble." She wiped the lipstick off my face, and then made her way into the mall.

After I dropped Angel off, I rode through my East Memphis neighborhood. I spotted my

partners. Terio Speed, and Lil Jake standing on the corner of Apple Blossom and

Flowering Peach. I parked my Cutlass in Terio's driveway and then joined them.

"What up Jinx?"

I greeted them both with love and a handshake. I passed Terio the blunt I was smoking.

"It's slow out here," I commented, knowing their block was usually jumping.

"It's a drought on the good work... That nigga Ziggy want a mu'fucker to pay $30,000 a brick. We're eatin' but not like that," Jake said.

Terio added to Jake's statement. "Plus, he ain't frontin' less than three of them bitches." He passed Jake the blunt. "He got a mu'fucker ready to rob his bitch ass." Terio laughed.

"That's what's up." I laughed. "I might have another angle though.

What does $25,000 sound like?"

Jake passed me the blunt. "Sounds like we need to talk in the house."

"Mane what, we can cop two right now," Terio added.

"You cop two and I'll front the same," I told them.

They looked at each other and smiled. "That's a deal."

I checked my watch. "It's 3:45. Y'all meet me at Icky's at six." I sealed the deal by shaking their hands and then I got in my car. As soon as I pulled off, I called Icky.

"What's up, brah? You still on your get down or lay down?"

"Always!" he replied.

"Good. I'll be out there in 30 minutes. I have an idea." I hung up.

Terio and Jake had given me an idea. We were robbing Ziggy.

Chapter 8
Lucky
"FORTUNE"

One week later

"The gray ones look good with that set. But I got a Hoyas set in the back that'll kill with the Jordan's, the sweat suit, and fitted cap. That'll be close to $400, but I can save you bout $60 on my discount."

Homey thought for moment. "Cool but you keep the $60," he said. "What they call you?"

"They call me Lucky."

He and I shook hands. "I'm Bad Boy. You're a good salesman...You should be running this place," he said.

"You think so?" I replied with pride.

"You convinced me... Where you from?" he asked.

"*B.H.Z.* I grew up in Tulane." I put his things in a bag after ringing him up. "You from the East Coast?"

He laughed. "I'm from East Memphis. Marina Cove; Winchester Sq., Knight Way, Willow Lake, Lake Point... I've been in New York for five years though, doing a Fed bid."

I took notice of the ink work covering his neck, arms, and hands. It was some excellent shit with lots of portraits. He raised his shirt. His entire upper body was done.

"I did 126 months-ten and a half years. Anyways, you ever made

$2500 in ten minutes?" He put five hundred on the counter and waited for my reply.

"No offense, but I'm not the D-boy type," I said.

He laughed. "Me neither." He gave me a business card and then grabbed his bag. "Ask around your hood about me, and then give me a call. The five hundred is for your time."

I watched him leave, placing the money and card inside of my pocket before my nosey ass manager spotted me.

When I got off work, I went straight home. It was shortly after 6 p.m., on a Saturday, and I'd made plans to hang out with one of my side chicks. I only came home to shower and change. I was drying off when Sugar Momma walked into my room and let me know Jinx had come by earlier.

"Gimme me some money." She watched me count the money I had laying on my bed.

"Ask that trick that put those hickies on your neck."

"Lorenzo Mario Mendes you'd better give your momma some money."

I counted her a couple hundred out. She noticed the card on the bed. Instantly, she picked it up and looked at it.

"Where'd you get this from?"

"The dude Bad Boy came up to Footlocker today."

She zoned out momentarily. "What did he look like? What did he say?"

"Asked if I made $2,500 in ten minutes and where I'm from. He looked like Tyrese. Do you know him?"

She sat on my bed and lit a cigarette and told me to give her the phone and roll a joint.

I gave her the phone, then did as she asked.

"Debbie, guess who your nephew met. Bad Boy ain't but one Buck Davis." She put the cigarette out once I gave her the joint. "Girl, you know Toya still has her soul food spot, and her and her damn cousin own JC's, and I forgot about The Honeycomb."

I listened to Sugar Momma. Toya was Bad Boy's wife.

She hung up. "Lucky, you don't remember Bad Boy?"

"Am I s'posed to?"

"He ran in the circle with Killer D. Him, Killer D, Big Curt, Mac Goo, Big Lou. He came up with a guy named Skip Nelson." She was blushing.

"Buck life in the State and sixty-three years with the Feds. He had some bank robberies and gun charges. He won an appeal after they found some hidden evidence. Hmp, when you talk to him, tell him I said hi."

I looked at her sashay out of the room. Something was up and the only way to figure it out was to call Bad Boy, which is exactly what I was going to do.

Icky

"THE TAKEOVER"

"Staci said the nigga Ziggy and Yellow Boy just got to the spot. As soon as she calls me back, we're moving in," Jinx said while loading his 9 millimeter.

"What he s'pose to have?" I asked. I sat behind the wheel of the stolen Impala we were using for a getaway car.

Jinx smiled. "Ten bricks, close to a hundred and fifty-thousand."

"A'ight is this about the paper or the pussy?" Hurk asked. I couldn't help but laugh at the way Jinx looked at big brah.

"If it's the paper we ain't got to shoot him. But I heard Staci got that pussy worth dying for. With those pretty lips, I believe it," I joked.

"Fuck both y'all. One thing's for sure and two things for certain, this move is about the money. As far as Staci goes, that's mine already." Jinx paused when his phone vibrated. It must've been Staci because all he did was listen before he hung up.

Once he hung up, he gave me the okay to pull off. We were parked a block away from Ziggy's spot in McKellar Woods. I drove into the complex and pulled around to the back, near the trash dumpsters. It was dark out and because it was cold, the complex was fairly quiet."A'ight it's just Gangster, Ziggy, and Yellow Boy. We g'on go in, lay they ass down, then roll the fuck out-no shots," Jinx looked at me and added. "No shots, Slick."

"They better cooperate then," I replied. The three of us masked up and carefully crept to the back door. I could see Yellow Boy and Gangster Greg on the patio smoking weed. Jinx gave the signal.

"Put your mother fucking hands up!" I said. I aimed my AR-15 at

Gangster. I knew he was armed and not afraid to try to get his pistol. Hurk quickly patted him down and cuffed him with the flex cuffs.

"Let's move," Hurk told Yellow Boy.

"Aye Y.B. Oh shit," Ziggy was so shocked he dropped the Pyrex container he was holding and put his hands in the air.

Jinx punched him in the face and then snatched him by the collar. "Where that cash at?" he growled while shoving the barrel of the .9mm in Ziggy's mouth.

Ziggy pointed towards the bedroom. I watched Hurk cuff and gag Yellow Boy, then I kicked the bedroom door in. Staci sat on the bed in her bra and panties, counting stacks of money.

"Bitch if you move or make a sound, I'll kill your vanilla ass." I pointed the chopper at her and she immediately started to cry and shake.

Jinx took control. "C'mere, shawty… Pack all your man's shit in these bags get that cocaine too sweetheart." He slapped her on her ass and smiled as she obeyed without hesitating.

"Y'all better kill me. You niggas must not know who I am," Ziggy said.

"Nigga fuck you," Hurk replied. "You don't need no bricks anyway. I'm buying a S-Type Jag with your shit," Hurk said with a devilish grin. "Aye bitch, hurry up!" he told Staci.

"I couldn't help myself. I had to stir the pot. You think we got time to run a train on lil mama?" I asked.

"Don't touch her!" Ziggy snapped.

Jinx punched him in the face until blood poured from his rose gold grill.

"C'mere," He snatched the bags from Staci, tossed them to me, then kissed Staci like he was trying to suck her face off. "You need to find a man that can keep your sexy self safe. Next time you might get more than a kiss and a pat on your cute lil ass. Let's roll fellas."

The three of us ran to our ride and were gone in a matter of seconds. "Woo! That shit was too mu'fuckin' easy," I yelled as I smashed off.

"We got nine bricks, close to $100,000," Jinx said.

"I saw how you were looking when I said something about fuckin' Staci. I saw how you were lookin'," I said. "Let me find out you soft on that nigga, bitch."

“Let's celebrate,” Hurk said.

I smiled. “I can't, Nyla's is pregnant I gotta go see her.”

“That’s what's up. Congratulations my guy. Shit, it's time to step your game up,” Hurk said.

“I know. Eat by any means and never get full. The life of a *Dinner Thief*. Now divide that shit up so I can drop you clowns off. Jinx with that nice ass robbery. You could've at least let me shoot that nigga in his ass cheeks.”

Chapter 9
Jinx
"THE ART OF SEDUCTION"

As soon as the bell sounded at 2:15, I was rushing out to my car. It was Friday, homecoming weekend, and I had business to handle.

First, I had to drive out to Terio's to drop off a package and pick up some money he and Jake owed. After that, I was supposed to ride through Raleigh to holler at Doll Baby, a hustler that Jake turned me on to. After I did that, I had to take Staci to the mall so that she could spend some of the money she helped me make when we robbed Ziggy.

Speaking of that, it had been a couple of days since it happened, and the city had started talking. I heard so many different stories, none of which implicated me or my guys so I wasn't too concerned.

"Jeremy." I'd just tossed my backpack in the truck when Dominique called my name. She and I hadn't been talking much, becoming more and more distant with each passing day.

"Damn you act like I'm just any old female."

I sat on the hood of my Cutlass after I started it. "I'm just giving you that space you needed to think. What's up though?"

She played with my diamond chain and smiled. "I want you to spend the night with me tonight… me, Xaviera, Ebony, Star, and Vida are going out. You can bring your boys if you're afraid."

I noticed Angel and Alicia as they waved at me from the far end of the parking lot. "I might be able to do that, even if I come alone," I told her.

"I just want some dick, you can still be mad when it's over, just take it out on my pussy." She kissed my lips, then rejoined her girls.

"What's up with that with that? You back in?" Lucky asked.

"Just for tonight. Anyway, I'm out. I'll meet y'all at the game."

I left the school and drove out to the east side. Jake was waiting on me. We made the quick exchange then I was off to The Bay to meet up with Doll Baby.

Initially, I wasn't willing to serve him, but after talking with the homegirls, Pasha and Cookie, I was convinced it would be wise. Doll Baby was Pretty Tony's right hand, second in command of the Pretty Boy Thugs. Pretty Tony was the leader, but Doll Baby was the one with the longest money. He usually got two or three bricks from Ziggy, but due to the drought in the amount of work for Ziggy, I was the one he was shopping with.

When I pulled into the driveway, I spotted a couple of females on the porch. I got out and asked them where Doll Baby was.

"He went to the corner store. He said he should be right back," one of them answered. "What's your name?" the snow bunny asked.

"They call me Jinx."

"You're Jinx Vaughn?" the other one asked.

I nodded and gave my usual cocky smirk. "How do you know me?"

"Boy please, Angel talks about you like you're the best thing smoking. You are cute though, I love your shoes," the snow bunny complimented my orange and tan Air Max 95 sneakers.

"I'm Kat," she said.

"I'm Tameka; Doll Baby is my brother," the other chick added.

Doll Baby's purple Charger pulled into the driveway. He parked and got out.

"My fault," he said to me. "Meka roll a couple of those blunts." He tossed her a box of cigarillos then followed me out to my car.

"That's two and a half, the half is on me," I said once we were inside. He reached into his pants and handed me a fat wad of cash.

"It's all there, all 55,000. I'll probably be calling you again on Monday, no later than Tuesday."

"That's cool, you got my number. Shit, tell your boy to get at me too, I heard he took a loss the other night." I said.

He laughed. "That's how the game goes. Anyway, I'll be in touch."

My phone rang before he got out. I saw it was Staci and got real cocky.

"What up Staci? You ready yet?"

"Yeah, you on your way?"

"As soon as I leave Doll Baby I am. Give me about 30 minutes." I hung up and smiled at Doll Baby. "That's how the game goes," I said as I gave him dap. He smiled knowingly and got out.

I left North Memphis and drove across town to Black Haven. Staci's fine ass was waiting, looking like a young Kim K. When I got to Whitehaven High, she was standing with her friends.

"I see you, Gucci jeans, Giuseppe Zanotti heels on. Hair in a french braid. A gangster gotta have long money fuckin' with your bad ass."

She kissed my lips as soon as she got in the car. "I missed you. Damn I want you all to myself," she flirted.

"You got me. Shit, I'm about to blow your ex-boyfriend's savings on your fine ass. You think I'm not all yours?

She laughed. "You know he accused me of setting him up. Gangster Greg blames Murder Mook and Yinka."

"Fuck both of them niggas. I'm a *Dinner Thief,* no plates are safe or off-limits."

"Eat then baby, get full."

I looked at her and smiled.

"I'll eat but I'll never get full, shawty. *Dinner Thieves* never get full, you dig!" I said boldly.

"I dig it booh. Now, let's go shopping so you can take me home and eat me, since you never get full."

Bounce

"STAMPED AND APPROVED"

"Aye Lil brah, what you bout to get into?"

I watched Jinx as he helped Staci into her car. I was under the impression that we were going over Dominique's, but the way Staci was smothering his ass had me second guessing that plan. He kissed Staci, and then watched her pull off.

"What's up. Y'all ready?" he asked.

"J.V let me find out you had to check with Staci," Lucky said.

"For what? I just love to see shawty smile. Anyway, I thought we were going over Nikki's?" He paused when he noticed Dominique and her girls approaching us.

"What's up!" Dominique asked Jinx. "I'll be ready as soon as this traffic dies down."

He looked at Lucky and me. "Yeah, I want to get some food first."

I was too busy staring at Ebony Young to reply. She was Gangster Greg's girl, a sexy model type with long hair and hazel eyes. Her and Vida were cousins, she was Star Cooper's best friend, and tonight she was my mission.

"Dang, how long are you going to eyeball me?" she asked after a moment or two.

"As good as you look I might look all night. What's up, you trying to go get something to eat?" I laid my back against my Cutlass and once again eye fucked her. Vida's hating ass whispered something to her, and then seconds later Gangster Greg appeared. He said he needed to talk to Jinx, but I could sense some tension between him and Ebony.

Jinx gave Dominique his keys, and then he walked off with Gangster who'd pulled Ebony along as well.

"So we're all going to eat?" Lucky's silly ass asked. He smacked Vida's ass and whispered something to her that she couldn't stop blushing about.

"I'm cool," I said. "I'll get with y'all tomorrow. Let J.V. know I'm out." I got in my car and pulled off. I hadn't even made it off the lot when my phone rang.

"Yeah," I answered.

"Give me some time, I promise it'll be worth it." It was Ebony on the other line.

"All you have to do is choose. I can handle Gangsta," I replied.

"We'll see. Anyway, I need to go. I'll call you tomorrow," she said before ending our call.

I hung up with a grin. *Yeah, I'll get shawty, fuck that nigga Greg! I'm a Dinner Thief, I'll take what the fuck I want.*

Chapter 10

Hurk

"BROTHERLY LOVE"

One week later

"Jinx, I fixed your plate. What do you want to drink?" Angel handed Jinx a plate, then smiled after he tasted her cornbread. Her and Alicia had cooked Sunday dinner; fried catfish, macaroni, cornbread, and a garden salad.

I thumped her forehead. "Where's my plate?"

"Alexis is fixing it, I'm only responsible for Amy and my booh." She kissed Jinx's cheek before she left the den. Jinx looked at me and smiled.

"You know she calls me every morning to wake me up and every night before she goes to bed." He continued to stuff his mouth.

"Jeremy your side chick is on the phone." Angel rolled her eyes and tossed Jinx his phone.

"Where's my lemonade?" he asked.

"Tell your slore to get it," she continued to curse him out in spanish as she walked away.

I got up and went to get my plate. Alicia handed me a plate and asked me to take it to my mom.

"Thank you." Mom kissed my forehead and smiled. "You look handsome. Did you get that job you were talking about?"

"Yeah, I work for the guy that owns *The Honeycomb.*"

"Bad Boy?" She put her plate on the table. "Anthony, please don't go to prison and don't make me bury you before I am a grandmother. I mean, I know you're grown, and you do work, but I know more than you think, especially when it comes to Mr. Buck Davis." She kissed my cheek and added, "don't make me lose my mind."

Amy ran into the room and sat next to our mom. Angel's face was still screwed up when she walked in.

"Mom why does Jeremy think my feelings are a joke... sitting in there on the phone, eating my food."

I kissed my sisters and my mom before I left the room.

Jinx was putting his coat on when I got to the living room. "Angel Monique," he yelled.

"What!" she snapped. He counted her a few dollars. "Take your sisters to get their nails done and quit rolling your eyes at me."

I snatched him out of the house. The two of us were headed to meet Lucky, Icky, and Bounce at *Toya's*.

He started his car and backed out of the driveway. "I need to take that nigga Fatts a four-way and I still owe Terio a couple of pounds of weed," he said.

"You decided what you gonna do about Buck?"

"I'm cool on that. I told you I'm working this sack," he replied. "Major Vaughn already tripping, I might as well keep on pushing." His phone rang "Yeah? Damn, I just left you and gave you hundred and gave you some money." He laughed and said, "but you aren't my girl... Bye Angel." He hung up still smiling.

"She's breaking you down... by the time she's 18, you'll be part of the family for real." I laughed when he turned his phone off. "Staci won't stand a chance," I said with a smile.

Jinx

"TAKE NOTICE"

It was nearly 9 in the evening when I left my guys at *Toya's*. We'd been asked to meet with Buck, but I honestly wasn't feeling him like that. I sat and listened, but after a while I left. Besides, I had money to collect and drugs to sell.

"I appreciate you. I know you ain't with all that ripping and running and shit." Fatts handed me the money for the four and a half ounces I'd just sold him. "Grover wanted me to get at you about a nine piece."

"Tell him it'll be $6750 let him know I'm ready when he is." I checked my watch. "I'm out though." He and I shook hands, then I got in my car and left.

Fatts lived in Orange Mound, on Semmes, not far from a neighborhood in South Memphis called Magnolia. I knew that a few more known hustlers hung out at a little spot on Wabash.

"Ain't it past your bedtime?" the big homey Gooch asked.

"Turn that loud shit down," Nacho added. Gooch and Nacho were the top dogs in Magnolia. I met them through Bounce's girl, Valencia.

I turned my car off and got out. Other than Nacho and Gooch, there were about 20 other guys in the parking lot of the club.

"What's up," I greeted them both as I zipped my blue polo coat. It was a chilly late October night, but from the looks of things, I was at the place to be.

"What you doing in the hood and you got school in the morning?" Gooch asked.

I lit a blunt and smiled. "I'm trapping, tryna to get on your level." "You got to have a few more birthdays lil homey. I've been hearing good things though."

"I'm just trying to do me." I scanned the crowd and noticed a familiar face. "Y'all got it poppin' out here," I said.

Nacho laughed. "It's always poppin'. One time!" he yelled as two cop cars pulled up. The crowd casually started to separate. I had over a stack in cash and over two ounces of coke, so you know I got my young ass in the car.

I was about to pull off when Cookie and Pasha got in. I noticed Cookie's pretty ass, and

though I didn't know Pasha's horse booty was there, it didn't surprise me that they

were together.

"What are you doing out on a school night? Your mean ass daddy is going to have you doing push-ups in the driveway," Pasha joked from the backseat.

I passed Cookie the blunt as I headed to her house. "I'm just out. What y'all got going on?"

"Youngblood had a show at *Club Memphis*. We just left there before we came here. Anyway, you know I'm mad at you."

I laughed. "Lil Mane volunteered to get put down," I said knowing what she was talking about.

"That's his business. I'm mad cause you didn't put me down too," Cookie replied.

"For real... I wanna be a Dinner Thief too," Pasha added after Cookie passed her the blunt.

"Ain't no females," I said.

"That's even better. We can be the first," Cookie added.

I sat at the stop light on Elvis Presley Blvd. and Person Street, right in front of Hamilton High.

"Y'all serious?" I asked. A smile spread across my face when I realized they were. "A'ight, but don't think I'm sparin' y'all. I'll beat y'all ass the same way I did Lil Mane."

"N'all booh, I don't think you understand." Cookie leaned over and slid her hand inside my baggy black jeans.

"Pussy g'on get us in."

Pasha laughed. "And you can fuck us however you choose."

"Well damn, I could've put y'all down years ago." I held Cookie's hand in my lap and smashed the gas as the light changed from red to green. “I love this gangster shit.”

“You ain't seen shit yet booh. Just wait until we get to the house," Pasha added confidently.

Chapter 11

Icky

"ITCHY TRIGGER FINGER"

Four months later

"Please don't forget to call me in the morning," Tierra massaged my shoulders as I put my shoes on. I came by her place to pick up a package for Terio Speed. She was one of the new chicks Jinx put down. Anyway, when I got to the house, her ass had just gotten out of the shower. We ended up fucking like rabbits.

I counted out a couple hundred and then kissed her face. "Buy your lil girl some Jordans. I'll call you in the morning." I smacked her ass. "Walk me to the door."

"You got some weed?" she asked.

I gave her the bag of kush I had on me. I was out and grabbed the backpack containing the quarter brick I'd come for and rushed out to my ride.

Tierra lived in Ridgecrest, a neighborhood I really wasn't familiar with, but cats knew what I was about, so when I walked out to my truck the locals got out of my way.

In the four months since hooking up with Buck, our street cred had shot through the roof. I was seeing so much money. I sold my Tahoe and was pushing a new candy red Navigator on 26's.

My role in the D.T.G. was that of a linebacker. I handled the dirty work but by choice of course. I loved being on the block, in the trap, making sure the soldiers stayed on point. I wasn't a drug dealer; I was the dude that cats paid so they could sell drugs.

On my way to Terio Speed's spot, I blasted Three 6 Mafia's *Mystic's Styles* album. I had the music so loud that my mirrors shook while I sat at the light on Mount Moriah and Mendenhall.

The only reason I noticed my phone was because the screen kept lighting up.

"Yeah," I answered.

"Icky, are you coming by the house?" I turned the music off. "Hey Nyla... Aye baby, I'll be there in an hour. I got to do something for Jinx."

"Okay bring me a sundae from Sonic."

"I gotcha... I love you."

She giggled. "You made your daughter kick. Anyway, I love you too, bye-bye.

I hung up with her, then dialed Speed's number. He answered and came outside after I let him know I was out there. *This big nose... Young Joc lookin'*, I laughed to myself.

He got in the passenger's seat. "Damn Slick you eating good. In this bitch looking like a fat Jeezy," he said.

We exchanged bags. "I'm just grinding. Anyway, just let brah know if you want some more work." I gave him a fake ass handshake, then turned my music back up once he got out of the truck.

On my way home I stopped and got Nyla's sundae. My shorty was due any day now and I was anxious. Nyla and I lived in the house I grew up in. Cool and her husband moved once they were married then Nyla moved in so she and I could raise our little girl under the same roof.

Baby, Hurk's on the phone."

I must've fallen asleep on the couch. "What's up G?" I asked grabbing the phone from my girl.

"Meet me at Cookie's."

I checked my watch. "Right now?"

"10 minutes ago." He hung up without another word.

"I let you sleep as long as I could," Nyla said. I kissed her after she gave me my keys.

"I'll be back in a little while." She told me to be careful as I headed out to my Crown Vic.

I lived on Greenwood, only two minutes from Cookie's house on

McLemore and Neptune.

"Icky, you need to let a real bitch ride that dick." One of the hood rats yelled from the apartment complex across the street. I ignored her as I walked on Cookie's porch.

"What's up G?" I greeted Hurk when I stepped inside. "Damn Pasha, that ass so big."

"Shut up." She got off the couch and headed towards the back room.

"You know Murder Mook robbed Shotgun?" Hurk passed me the weed he was puffing on. I led the way out of the house. Shotgun was one of our guys from Orange Mound-you don't violate a *Dinner Thief* unless you want a war.

Murder Mook and his crew hung out in Gaston Park, only a few streets over. I drove straight there, spotting them as I drove by. He was with two of his boys, posted on the basketball court in the center of the park.

I parked on the curb, got out, and started shooting at them like I was John Wayne. I squeezed off 17 shots, firing until all three of them fell. I walked up on them, change clips and laughed while they tried to crawl to safety. "*Dinner Thief Gangsters*… fuck the Wolfpack, you hear me boy! *D.T.G.* And I'm in the hood every day."

Bounce

"#1 FAN"

"Welcome to *The Honeycomb*, where every Saturday night is 21 and under and ladies free before 10 P.M. shout out to the *Dimes and Divas*. I see you Miss Ebony Young, Happy Birthday. What up Vida... Star... *Pretty Boy Thugs* in this bitch too. Pretty Toney, Doll Baby," Yellow Boy gave his shout outs all over his new track.

I was seated at the table with Lucky and Jinx enjoying the vibes and watching the action.

It was a full house partly because of the three-dollar admission, but also because of Ebony's birthday party.

"That bitch so sexy," Lucky said. We were both watching Ebony on the dance floor. She wore a pair of tight white jeans, a fitted pink sweater, and matching stilettos. She was stunting too. She wore her hair up so the *D.T.G.* tattoo on her neck was visible. Me and her had been doing our thing on the low for about three months. She was still with Gangster Greg, I was with Valencia, but since the night Jinx and I put her and Vida down she's been mine.

"Gangster must not be here," Lucky said.

Jinx motioned towards the pool table. "He's over there. You know cats too cool to recognize when their girl ain't theirs. She's on Bounce, ya dig." He saluted me and smiled.

"I'm just glad I got a chance to hit once. My boy got a dime and a diva... Shawty in magazines, ridin' M-3 BMW."

"Why she with that fat ass, fake ass albino rhino then?" Lucky asked.

"Cause he paying what he weighs." I got up and made my way to Ebony. I was ready to give her the gift I bought. She smiled, but Star rolled her eyes. She was *D.T.G.* too. Lucky and Jinx put her down and though we used to mess around, it was Ebony I wanted.

"Hi handsome. You g'on put that pink necklace around my neck or do you want to dance?" Ebony flirted while grooving to Usher's *Lovers and Friends*.

"What about your boyfriend?" I put the necklace on for her. She took my white Yankee fitted off of my head and placed it on her own, then she pulled me out to the center of the dance floor. Chris Brown's *Poppin* played as we did our thing. The two of us put on a show too, moving like Chris Brown and Ciara. Yeah, I was a gangster but I could dance my ass off -all my guys could to.

"Bitch, what's your problem?" Gangster Greg snatched her arm and led her to a dark corner. She jerked away and told him to leave her alone.

I stepped between them.

"Aye Gangster, chill out." He mean mugged me like he wanted to knock me out. I knew he wasn't a coward, but he knew I wasn't scared of him either. Plus, he witnessed me shoot that pistol and I always had it too.

"Aye Bounce, c'mon G we fuck with Gangster," Jinx said calmly.

I looked at Ebony. "You cool?"

She smiled. "I'll be right there," she said.

I walked to the table with Jinx and Lucky. "My fault," I told them once I sat down.

"That pussy got you," Lucky said. We laughed until Jinx spotted Icky enter the club. He was dressed in all white, wearing so many chains he looked like a rapper in a video.

"That fool thinks he's Young Jeezy," Lucky said. "You know he shot Murder Mook, Ying-Yang, and Hump.We gotta stay on point, ya dig."

I watched Ebony approach the table. She greeted Jinx and Lucky, then sat on my lap. "Let's go," she said. "I have a room at the Adam's Mark and I want you to spend the night with me."

"I'm out y'all." I showed my guys love, then led Ebony out to my black on black Q-45.

Yeah I'd upgraded, from the Cutlass to an Infiniti, and from a girl to a diva, ya dig.

Chapter 12
Jinx
"THE CHOSEN ONE"

Valentine's Day

"N'all, I just left my lil young bitch, I'm on the way to drop Staci's gift off." I started my truck and turned the heat on before I pulled out of Tameka's driveway.

"Just make sure you don't forget to pick me up while you're visiting your bitches.

Anyway, I have to go." Angel hung up on me.

It was a snowy Valentine's Day Eve and I was making my rounds. I'd taken Dominique to breakfast, a movie, and a Tennessee Vols sweater dress since she's committed to play ball for the Lady Vols. We weren't dating anymore, but I still had feelings for her so I had to make her smile.

Since the day I met her, Tameka and I had been talking. I got her a cute Gucci set, a pair of heels, and a teddy bear. Staci's position in my life was different. The streets knew what the jewelry box on her calf represented, just like I knew how she'd earned the *Dinner Thief* tattoo in the small of her back. Shawty was my prize jewel, ya dig.

When I got to her home in Whitehaven, I parked underneath the carport, right next to her maroon Mercedes. Her folks spoiled her because she was an only child and a straight A student. I learned quickly that she was materialistic, but she wasn't a gold digger just because she was used to having her way.

"Ohh... Hi baby, I love your sweater," she greeted me on the porch with a hug and a kiss, complimenting my pink and gray polo sweater. "You got your Cam'ron look working. You actually wore the gray and pink Forces I bought," she added.

I sniffed her hair. "You smell good. Make a gangster wanna eat your fine ass." I bit her collarbone until she had a dark red passion mark on her cocoa butter colored skin. Her body was so soft, titties sat perfectly, and her butt fit her body well too. Lil mama was one of those exotic

types, and you knew she was the shit.

"Stop." She giggled when I continued to tease her.

"You g'on fuck around and get a baby." I followed her up to her bedroom and rested in the middle of her bed. She climbed on top of me and took her hair out of the french braid it was in.

"Guess what I did today?"

"I hope you went to the spa and let the lil Asian girls pamper you."

She emptied my pockets the way she always did, counting my cash afterwards. "Guess," she whined while deleting the calls and texts that weren't from her phone.

"You called and texted me all day," I replied. She laughed while helping me out of my sweater.

"I went to Victoria's Secret. You want to see what I got just for you?"

"Let me get your gift first."

She let me up. I walked into her closet and got the gift I'd hidden two weeks prior. She blushed at the sight of the Giuseppe Zanotti boots and matching pink and red YSL sweater and knee length skirt. "Ohh... I'm wearing these for homecoming this weekend." She held the skirt up to her waist and stood in the mirror.

"Damn, these boots are so sexy! Show all your hoes my tat."

I counted my money, then took my watch off. It was 7:17 p.m., I still had almost 2 hours to kill.

Her phone rang. "Hello... hey Ziggy." She put her gift in the closet.

I pulled her back to my chest and softly kissed her on her neck. I didn't give a damn about her boyfriend being on the phone. Staci Capri Armstrong was mine, not his. "I was going. Well, if it was important you'd be here, not in Atlanta with Yellow Boy." She bit her bottom lip when I slid my hand underneath her

Tweety Bird sweatshirt. Her nipples were hard already, probably from the butterfly kisses on her neck.

I laid her on the bed and spread her thighs. “You better hang up.”

“Ziggy... I'll call you back.” She hung up and pleaded for me to make her cum. In a matter of seconds, we were both naked and under her covers.

“Jeremy... I want a girl,” she whispered- her way of telling me not to put on the rubber I was about to open.

I looked into those gray eyes and pushed my hips forward until my rod parted her opening. She came as soon as I was all the way in. We made love until we were both in a deep sleep.

If Angel hadn't called I probably would've still been asleep beside Staci. The entire 30 minute drive from her house to Angel's job my mind was racing- Staci's love had never felt better! It took two blunts to calm me down.

When I got to the mall, Angel and one of her coworkers were standing in front of Macy's. I could tell by her angry, bowlegged walk that Angel was mad.

“My fault,” I said as soon as she got in.

She rolled her eyes. “Can you take her home? She lives behind Wooddale Middle.”“You hungry?” I asked, attempting to smooth things over.

“Just take me home,” Angel mumbled.

“I told you my fault. Shit, I got caught up. I ain't but five or ten minutes late.”

“What the fuck ever. Shit, take us home. Then take your ass back to whoever had you five or ten minutes late.” She pulled her phone out. “Hey Alexis, is Momma home? What about big brother? Just you and Amy? N’all Jinx.”

I looked at her friend through the rearview mirror and asked if she smoked. When she said yes I passed her a blunt to fire up.

“Alexis want some doughnuts and she said don't forget it's Valentine's.” Angel hung up the phone, and then toyed with my stereo.

“I got her and Amy covered.”

“Hmp... It figures, everybody comes before me.”

I didn't respond, not another word. Even when I dropped her friend off, I just drove, stopping only to get what Alexis wanted me to bring her. It wasn't until after I filled my gas tank up that I said anything.

"Get that bag from behind your seat. That's your gift." I pulled into traffic. I noticed how Angel's expression changed when she grabbed the bag.

She tried to fight it, but the sight of the white teddy bear, the card, the box of turtles, and the dozen red roses crushed all that angry shit.

"Thank you but I'm still done with you. I'm tired of having my heart broken. I'm far too arrogant to keep chasing you."

"Angel, we aren't a couple. You're like a lil sister to me."

She rolled her eyes. "Please, miss me with that lil sister shit. I know you want me just as much as I want you. Hell, you think I don't notice how you look at me or how hard you try not to smile when I call you to check on you, or remind you to pick up your money from people. Shit, fine as I am, I know you feelin' me. Your ass is just scared."

I turned into a vacant lot and parked my truck.

"What do you want from me? I try my best to be one hundred percent with you but you ain't understanding. You're not on my level. I don't have time for no lil girl shit."

Fop! She slapped me, and then got out of the truck.

"I hate you. I hope you get what you deserve too. Sissy bitch, don't call me no damn lil girl."

I snatched her and she slapped my ass again. I pinned her back on the truck and held her while she kicked, kneed, and punched. I don't know why, but to calm her down, I kissed her. I mean, I kissed her as if she was the key to life. And when she responded by kissing me back, I felt myself loving it. Before I realized it, I opened the back door, and pushed her skirt up past her waist.

"Oh my God, Jinx." She squeezed my dick through my jeans.

"Shut the fuck up." I went face first between her thighs and licked through her panties - a sexy purple thong! I'd only given four females head; Sugar Momma, Lucky's aunt, his sister and Staci. But once I tasted Angel I was sprung.

She mumbled in Spanish and scratched my scalp while I did my thing.

"What are you doing to me," she cried. "Oh Jeremy thank you!" she cried.

"You want me to stop?"

She pulled me on top of her and wrapped her legs around me. "Please Jeremy... please make love to me... I want you to be my first," she begged.

"Happy Valentine's Day, Angel." I slipped the rubber on, then spent the next two hours slowly and lovingly breaking Angel in. I gave her the gift she'd been waiting for until she couldn't take it anymore.

Chapter 13

Icky

"PROUD DADDY"

Two weeks later

Jinx approached me with a Macy's bag in his hand and a proud smile his face. I was standing outside the nursery, watching my baby sleep peacefully.

"Which one is my niece?"

"In front of us. Koby N'shell Turner... 8 pounds 7 ounces."

"Congratulations big brother." He handed me a bag and showed me love. "I gotta take

Val some work. Do me a favor when you leave here, holler at Sandman for me.

"Keep it though. Put it in Koby's college fund."

After he left, the nurse let me take Koby into Nyla's room.

"She's your twin," I told Nyla as she held our daughter. "You cool?"

"I'm fine I can't wait to take her home though."

I smiled. "I gotta do a lot of changing... Can't be getting' high at home no more. Can I ask you a question?"

"What is it?"

I rested my head on her thigh.

"You wanna marry me?"

"Are you serious? You know I want to marry you," she said with a huge smile. "Where is my ring?"

The two of us shared a long kiss to seal the deal we just made. I stayed at the hospital until Nyla fell asleep. When I left, I headed to North Memphis to handle the business Jinx asked me to take care of.

"What up?" Sandman met me on the porch and led the way inside of the trap house him and Ace hustled out of. They were in the heart of North Memphis, on Vollintine, directly across the street from North Side High School. The spot was jumping too.

"What's up?" I noticed Star laying on the couch. "Damn Star, you got that fat ass poking out them boy shorts. In this bitch lookin' like Nicki Minaj." Sandman gave me a funny look after I showed Star love, she was *D.T.G* too.

"C'mon to the back," Sandman said.

Star gripped her ass cheeks and smiled while I followed Sandman. That bitch was scandalous, the type that would set a sucker up for the okey doke. She had a rep that was well deserved. The bitch was dangerous but I was digging it. I knew she was fucking Ace, but she was in the spot with his right-hand man.

"I got $3500, Ace has the other half. Let Jinx know we need half a brick though."

I counted the cash. "I'll front you a nine, but brah ain't g'on fuck with Ace til I get that lil paper."

"Shit I guess I'm good with that," he said with a smile. "I can meet you at the Raleigh Mall at six tonight."

The two of us headed back up front. Star had put on a pair of red tights and a sweatshirt. She asked me to drop her off over her brother's house. One look at that donkey butt and you know I said yes.

"Ace was supposed to take me, but he with my brother and Fred Wooten."

I pulled out of the driveway. "When you talk to him, let him know I need my money. Fuck around and make me hunt him down."

"That nigga ain't gettin' no money."

"That's why you laid up with his partner?"

She sucked her teeth, and then smiled. "My pussy gets hot sometimes. Let's just say Sandman doesn't mind sucking it until it cools off. Plus, he pays well."

"Fat as that pussy is I bet it does get hot."

"Don't hate. Anyway, I heard Nyla had her baby."

I smiled proudly. “Yeah, her name's Koby. What’s up with you though?”

“All work, gangster shit, ya dig?”

I smiled. “Oh yeah... you need some help?”

“You think your booh can handle me and you helping each other.”

“Ain't but one way to find out.” I unzipped my jeans. “We can start with a shot of that face though.”

She put her blue hair in a ponytail and smiled. “I thought you’d never ask.”

Yeah, it was official, with Star on my team I was back on my bullshit. I had a family now; no one outside my circle was safe- I was taking all plates.

Bounce

"NOTHING SEEN, NOTHING SAID"

"Aye brah, let me holler at you right quick," I whispered to Jinx as he stood on the curb with his arms around Staci's waist.

I walked over and sat on the hood of my car while I waited for him. My nerves were on edge. Icky and some of our guys from Orange Mound were involved in a shootout. The homeboy Shotgun was killed.

Jinx sat next to me. "What's up?"

"Somebody rode through The Mound and punished Shotgun. Icky was with him."

"I just took brah a four-way about two hours ago. He was with Lil Mane in Melrose Park." Jinx shook his head in disbelief. "I'll ride through and check on his sister."

Icky's Crown Vic came flying down the street. He parked and jumped out with the motor still running.

"Aye brah, that nigga Super Dave merked brah. Hit my nigga with the AK."

"Shit, that's what it is then. We at the whole Wolfpack. Matter fact, I'm 'bout to take Staci home." Jinx showed us love.

"Nothing seen, nothing said," I said. It was understood. Whoever spotted a member of the Wolfpack would shoot on sight. "I'm s'posed to pick up Catera. Don't forget we have that meeting with Buck tomorrow."

"Fuck Buck," Jinx said as him and Staci left.

"Why brah don't like your sister's baby daddy?" Icky asked me. He pulled out a powder pack and offered me some. I declined. "Damn Buck got your sister pregnant in prison?"

“He said Buck is up to something. My sister won’t talk about how she got pregnant. I fuck with Buck though, all this paper we seein'. Plus, he put me on Catera.”:

“You fuck her old ass yet?”

“She only but 28 but yeah, I fucked the first night.”

I spotted a dark colored SUV creeping down the block. We were at Val's house, on Victor Street, her spot set on the top of the hill so I noticed the masked men inside the Explorer.

Pop! Pop! Pop! Pop! Pop!

I fired first, then Icky followed suit. The SUV returned fire, then sped off seconds later.

“Fuck! Them niggas almost caught us slippin'!” Icky said.

Val and Smurf came out of the house. “What the fuck was that?” Val asked.

“Some stupid niggas with death wishes,” I replied with a cold tone. It was official, we were at war. We didn’t have the numbers but we were well prepared for battle.

Chapter 14
Hurk
"ANYTHING GOES"

One week later

"Big brother, Angel has a jewelry box tattoo on the back of her neck." Alexis yelled as she rushed into my bedroom. "Yeah, I caught her and Jinx kissing the other night too."

I was playing Connect Four with Amy. "Momma knows about the tattoo. And I punched Jinx in the stomach already."

"Ugh, I can't wait til I turn sixteen so I can kiss Lucky." She rolled her eyes and left the room.

I tickled Amy after she beat me. "You cheated!" She ran out screaming that she'd beaten me. I followed her down to the den. "Alicia, what time y'all going to the game?"

"I'm ridin' with Smurf and Birdie. Angel's waiting on Jinx."

Angel walked in and kissed my cheek before she helped Alicia fix her hair. "I'm ridin' with momma, Amy, and Alexis."

"Brah must be taking Staci?" I asked her. She put her hand on her hip and looked me up and down.

"She's driving her own car. My booh has to meet some dude named I-40. He'll be there by the halftime of the girls' game."

I knew I-40 was Jinx's coke connect, but I'd found out from Buck that I-40 was only a middle man. Him and Vago worked for a guy from Chicago named Cappie Loyd- Buck's cellmate in the prison.

"Call him," I told Angel. She told me he was with Lucky, and then passed me her phone.

"Didn't I tell your spoiled ass I'll see you at the game," he answered, obviously assuming I was Angel.

"It's me brah. Aye, did you talk to Bad Boy?"

"Fuck Buck. That's y'all guy, I'm not cool with the role model thing," he replied. "Anyway, don't forget to stop by Slick's. Leave what he gives you for me in your car. I'll get it at the game."

"Aight."

"Aye brah put Angel on the phone for me."

I gave her the phone, got my keys, and then left. Thirty minutes later I was walking into Icky's living room. He was playing with his daughter while Nyla curled her hair.

"What up big brother? Your Curtis Jackson lookin' ass." He got up and showed me love.

"Aye Nyla, this fool got all this green and gold on. Full of school pride."

"They g'on lose. Everybody knows Hamilton has the best boys and girls team." The two of them laughed. Icky transferred to Hamilton so he could be close to Nyla. "Change her while I talk to brah. I'll be ready to go in ten minutes," he told her. He led me out the backdoor and out to the garage.

"Brah, you know how much work Buck gave us. Fifty bricks, ten each. What the fuck Buck got going? I ain't but scared but I ain't eighteen. I ain't tryna go to the Feds."

"I can't believe you're scared. I thought you wanted this."

He gave me my bag and Jinx's bag. "I have a lil girl brah. Me and Nyla getting married on prom day. Shit, my daddy and brother in the Feds. Boney is on the run and Diego too. I stay in some shit already, you and Bounce too. Shit, you shot at Super Dave two days ago."

I smiled. "I love it though. I tell you what, me and Jinx will get yours off and pay you for 'um. After this we'll do all of yours."

He handed me his bag too. "You sure?"

"Yeah fifteen bricks, I can flip my Maxima to a Jag or a Benz before spring break. And you know Jinx would love some extra money." I tossed the bags in my trunk once we were back in the front of the house. My instincts kicked in when I spotted a black SUV. Several shots came towards us causing us to scramble for cover.

"Fuck, I'm hit in my hip and my calf. Go check on Nyla and Koby. I need to get out of here."

I crawled to my car and sped off. I was hurt, but I wasn't stupid, I had to get to Pasha and Cookie's to drop the bags off, then and only then would I go to the hospital.

Lucky

"LUCKY'S LADIES"

"Umm... that was so amazing. I should cut your tires more often," Kourtney laughed after she pulled her panties over her vanilla covered ass. I'd originally came by her house to talk to her about our baby. She was three months pregnant, but when I told her about Iysis being two months pregnant, she slashed the tires on my Malibu.

I smiled as I watched her move around the room. For a snow bunny, Kourtney had a hood type of swagger. Aside from the fact that she was physically flawless, she was a nympho.

"You know I'm putting you on child support," she said with a slick grin.

I got out of the bed and went into the bathroom to clean myself up. "You act like I'm not going to take care of my baby."

"No, I'm just looking out for our baby and I'm not giving you anymore pussy."

I pulled my boxers and jeans up while she changed the sheets on her bed. Her comment wasn't worth a reply. We both knew I was the only cat hitting that pink taco between her legs.

My phone rang. "Yeah, this Lucky," I answered.

"Aye brah, Hurk got shot."

I grabbed my keys and hurried to put my shirt and shoes on. "When? Who did it?" I asked.

"Mo-B. He got hit in the hip and the calf. We up here at Baptist East."

"Aye Slick, I'm on my way G."

"Nothing seen- nothing said," he replied before hanging up.

Kourtney followed me to the car. "What's wrong?"

"Hurk got shot. I'll call you when I find out something else." I kissed her nose, and then left without another word.

I dialed Bounce's number on my way to the hospital. When he answered, he was just as mad as I was. He told me to call Buck and let him know what was up, so I did.

"What's up my boy?" Buck asked.

"Hurk got shot," I told him.

"Damn. A'ight, where is he?"

"Baptist East," I replied.

"Okay, I'll handle it. Call me as soon as you know how serious it is. Lucky, make sure you tell your brothers I'll handle it."

"I got'cha old school." I hung up. *Yeah, niggas can't know who they fuckin' with. Bad Boy g'on make them respect it though, all we gotta do is keep gettin' this paper.*

Chapter 15

Jinx

"NEVER GET FULL"

"C'mere...Jeremy," Vida called me as I was walking to my car. She was with Smurf and Birdie at her car. School had just let out, it was Friday, and I had too much to accomplish to waste time. Vida Ingram was a waste of time to me, especially with Angel and Staci running me crazy. I threw up the *D.T.G* at her, Smurf, and Birdie as I tossed my books into my car.

"I'm on G-shit. I know it ain't like that," Vida snapped.

"What you talkin' about?" I asked. I showed each of them love.

"Mo-B and Super Dave shot Hurk. They wanted to get you and Icky too. They said something about y'all robbing Murder Mook and Gangsta G a while back."

Angel and Alicia exited the gym and walked over to my car. I couldn't help but smile when I noticed the look Angel gave me. "I appreciate that. I owe you," I said to Vida. "You going to work today?"

She smiled. "I'm off, but I'll be at *The Honeycomb* if you want to see me."

"I see you now," I said, letting her know I wasn't trying to fuck her. "I'll stop through later so I can give you something for your help." I gave them love and then walked back to my Cutlass.

Angel punched me in my chest as soon as I got in the car. "I told you about that fish mouth duck."

"Chill out. You already got Staci sweating me about these scratches."

I rubbed the back of my neck.

"Well, I'm marking my territory. Next time I'm leaving my scent on you." She flirted, rubbing my face and purring like a cat.

Alicia laughed. "You should've seen how mad she had Dominique at lunch talking about how her booh got a new tattoo and cum constantly rubbing that jewelry box on her neck."

"Well, that hoe act like she's still in the picture." She kissed my lips, then started messing with my radio.

My phone rang as I turned into traffic. It was Staci calling to see if I was still spending the night with her. Her folks were out of town for the weekend. "I'll meet you at the club. You don't have to drive. Is that cool?" I asked.

"It's cool baby. Anyway, I'm driving now so I'll let you go. I love you."

I cut my eyes at Angel, knowing she knew who I was on the phone with. "I love you too. I'll see you tonight." I hung up and tossed my phone in Angel's lap.

"Don't make me hurt you," she said.

I leaned over and kissed her cheek. "I like it when you get kinky."

"Please hurry up and drop me off." Alicia laughed.

"Call Jake and tell him to meet me at the mall in fifteen or twenty minutes," I told Angel. She did as I instructed.

"Jinx, you and big brother doing good. You make me want to get put down," she commented. "I know one thing, y'all need to get whoever shot him."

"No doubt," I said. "Anyway, if you wanna get put down, I'll let Val and Cookie know."

Angel hung up my phone. "He said you still owe him a baby from last week." She answered my phone. "Who is this?" She covered the phone. "It's Yellow Boy. He said he wants the usual, but he needs it ASAP."

"Tell him to meet me at Lucky's in an hour."

"He said okay." She hung up, then turned to her twin. "You want to go shopping tomorrow?"

"We don't get paid until next week," Alicia replied. Angel reached over and grabbed my crotch.

"My baby is going to make sure we have something to wear to the Chris Brown show on Sunday. Alexis is coming too."

I did some quick math in my head. *$3,250 from Jake, $12,500 from Yellow Boy. Plus the $1600 I have on me. "$17,350,"* I said to myself. I hadn't even started working and I've already made a little money.

"How much of my money you trying to spend?" I looked over at Angel. She just smiled, letting her well-manicured french tips roam over my hardness. "Keep on playing," I said when she removed the sixteen hundred from my pocket. "Don't go broke before Monday."

"Jinx, you know Fish likes me?" Alicia asked. Angel gave her a couple hundred dollars. "Anyway, I might see what's up with him," she added after putting the cash in her purse.

"Bounce and Lucky helped me put brah down. Give him a chance and see what's up.Hell, he's playin' at Memphis next year, fuck around and he'll go pro."

I turned into the mall parking lot. "Don't call me all night Angel Monique." I kissed her lips. "Aye, Licia, get that money from that white boy at Footlocker. It's three hundred and fifty and you can keep it."

"Be careful," they said as they headed to work. I sat in the lot until Jake's white Explorer pulled next to my Cutlass. "I 'preciate you my guy. I'm down to my last little half ounce." He tossed me the money he owed.

"Aye… on the other half ounce I owe you, will you take an ounce of kush for it. I couldn't get to my spot to get that shit."

He laughed. "That's cool. Monday or Tuesday I'm trying to get a nine piece."

"You get money and I'll front you what you buy." I showed him love. "I told you brah, you're a Dinner Thief now, you will eat well!"

He laughed, looking like Paul Wall with all his platinum and diamond teeth showing. "Let me roll then so I can get that paper."

My phone vibrated while he was pulling off. It was Vago calling to let me know he was

in the city. He asked me to meet him and I-40 in an hour. Of course I let him know I'd be there.

I'd just hung up when I spotted a red and white Dodge Charger parked at the gas station next to the Oak Court Mall. *Oh shit, must be my lucky day... Mo-B and that pussy ass Super Dave*. I reached inside my stash spot and got my gun. I got out and cautiously crept behind cars until I was in a better firing range.

Dock! Dock! Dock! Dock! Dock! Dock! Dock! Dock! Dock! Dock!

The first three shots dropped Dave, the next three dropped Mo-B, and the rest were aimed at the tires of the Charger. While the rest of the people ran to their vehicles, I calmly crept back to my car. I pulled off, making sure I rode through the lot of the gas station so my victims would see my face. I wasn't hiding nor was I concerned about retaliation. I was a gangster, point blank period.

Lucky

"BIG SPENDER"

I pulled in front of Iysis' house in my brand new Celtic green S550. She was on the porch with her girls. I was on the phone with Bounce so I didn't get out because he was telling me about Jinx.

"Yeah, he called my sister to come down to *201*, but she said since it's Friday, he'll be there over the weekend. He only had some weed and like fifteen stacks on him. He'd just left my house." Bounce informed me.

"The cops are askin' about the shooting at the mall." He laughed. "Mo-B and Super Dave got hit," he added. Iysis stepped off the porch looking like a red-haired video vixen with an ass so fat I could see it from the front.

"Aye, I'm still going to the club, but I need to take Iysis this little money," I said before hanging up.

I got out and smiled while the people "ooh'd" and "ahh'd" at the sight of my ride. Plus, I had on an exclusive red and green Gucci set with the matching boots and fitted cap. Iysis lived on one of South Memphis' most popular blocks, Kerr and Mississippi. D-boys, hood rats, pimps, and hoes were all out and all eyes were on me, as they should've been.

"Damn girl, if you weren't already pregnant I'd put a baby in you. Out here with these tight ass jeans on. You know that ass stupid fat!" She moaned when I kissed her lips and grabbed two handfuls of booty meat.

"You ballin' today, looking like French Montana. C'mere, let me show you something in the house," she said.

Five minutes later, I was balls deep inside of Iysis, hitting that pregnant pussy like it was the key to life.

"Right there Lucky… harder. That's it." She was face down on the bed with all that ass in the air, throwing it at me like the pro she was. We both came so hard that we rolled over and fell asleep.

I woke up an hour later and took a quick bath. Iysis was still asleep so I left her money on the nightstand. It was pitch black outside, but the block was still jumping. I stood on the porch and smoked a bag of kush with Lil Mane and a few of his youngsters, and then I left.

My stomach was growling so I went to *Toya's* to get the Friday's catfish and spaghetti special. Buck and a couple of his guys were seated at the table in the back. I ordered and then joined them.

"What's up OG," I greeted him.

"Damage control. Lucky, this is Big Lou and Mac Goo. This is Lucky, Sugar Mama's baby boy." They both looked at him, then smiled like they had a secret.

"Boy your mom is my mu'fucker," said Mac Goo.

"Yeah, a nigga owe her a lot of big favors," Big Lou added.

"How y'all know her?" I asked.

Buck smiled. "Not like that. But, Sugar Momma hasn't always been as calm as you know her. She was a gangster before she had your sisters." He paused until the waitress brought my food and left again.

"You heard from Jinx? Hurk told me what happened. I know how your little brother is." He seemed irritated. "He's hardheaded and stupid. I also know violence is bad for business.

"That was retaliation," I said in between bites of my catfish.

"I told you I'd handle it." I could sense the anger in his voice, but more so in his eyes.

"You should've told him then," I replied honestly.

Mac Goo laughed. "Gooch said that little gangster goes hard. I saw him beat Murder Mook's ass a few months ago," Big Lou added. "And you know the Mexicans love him," Goo said.

"They don't run shit." Buck bit his lip, then continued. "Listen, when you hear from him, let him know I need to talk to him ASAP."

"I'll tell him, but that don't mean he'll listen."

"Then I'll just have to get his attention my own way," Buck replied. He tossed a twenty on the table then left.

Mac Goo and Big Lou smiled. "Take it easy lil brah," Big Lou said.

"Tell your momma and your aunt what's up," Mac Goo added.

I laughed to myself once they were gone. *Buck must not know, Jinx doesn't care about that shit he talkin'. That's Major Vaughn's tough ass son... Fuck around and Jinx g'on shoot his ass to*

Chapter 16
Jinx
"PLAY ON PLAYA"

Three days later

I'd only been out of jail for couple of hours, but already I was back at it again. After my court appearance and listening to Major Vaughn telling me how big of a disappointment I was,

I was making up for lost time. Hell, it cost me the fifteen racks I had the night I was arrested and I was being questioned about Mo-B and Super Dave's shooting.

"Aye Jinx, we're out of sandwich bags," Lil Mane said when he joined me on the porch.

"Pasha, go get some for me. Cookie, you need to make sure we always have some. Lil Mane, cook another 4-way. Serve everybody with green money. Everything must go." I tossed the bundle of ones into the yard and smiled as the kids ran to claim what they could.

I stepped off the porch and got in my new tan and champagne Escalade. I'd bought it an hour after I was released, trading in the Malibu. I pulled off blasting Rocko's *Dis Morning*.

Money wasn't the only thing on my mind. I was high and just as horny. Staci was on her period, Angel was sick with a nasty stomach virus, and I wasn't in the mood for Dominique's games. It had been a while since I heard from Buck's daughter so I called her.

She answered immediately. "Damn, what's up jailbird."

"You got jokes."

"Yep… Anyway, what you call me for? I thought you didn't have time for the bullshit dealing with Buck's daughter would cause"

I laughed, knowing I told her those exact words only a couple of months earlier. "I don't, but I have to be real, I'm trying to make time for Buck's daughter to put them yellow thighs on my sideburns, ya dig."

"Damn...just like that."

"I'm too gangster for the games."

She was quiet momentarily. "Where you at?"

"In route," I replied.

"I'll meet you at my school in thirty minutes." She hung up.

I'd been sitting in the parking lot of Germantown High for at least ten minutes when August pulled up in her white on white Range Rover. She got out of her truck and got into mine. The first thing I noticed was the short ass denim skirt she had on; she and I were on the same page.

"Damn, you got them sexy legs exposed looking like Ashanti and shit." She was blushing so hard when I sniffed her neck. I loved the vanilla body wash she had on.

"Drive around to the golf course. Anyway, what made you call me?"

I lit a blunt and adjusted my air vents and stereo. "I told you, I wanna suck you dry."

"You are crazy. I heard you tried to kill two people. How'd you get out so fast?"

I passed the blunt and clarified her statement. I let her know I was only locked up for a weed charge, but also that if I was trying to kill two people, two people would be dead.

"You are too fine to be so damn wild."

"Good girls love a bad guy, that's why you're in my truck." She passed the blunt to me and then pointed to the spot in the lot where she wanted me to park. We continued to smoke and listen to R. Kelly singing about 12 play. I could sense her nerves subsiding; her body language was more relaxed than it was when she first got into the truck.

"I thought... I thought you wanted to eat me out," she said almost in a whisper.

I didn't even say anything, I let my actions speak for me. I let my seat all the way back, and then pulled her on top of my face. Inside I was laughing, thinking about all the times Sugar Momma, Lucky's Aunt

Debbie, and his sister, Maria, had sat on and rode my face. August had no clue, but I ate pussy like Pac-Man ate those little white dots.

"Oh my... Ooh my Jesus! What are you doing? That's my... Oh you got your tongue in my ass."

I held her ass open and blew in it. The entire time she'd been with me, I been popping certs into my mouth. The cool mint and the warmth of my breath had her cumming, screaming, and begging for exactly what I knew she wanted from day one, some thug loving.

I licked and sucked her clit, fingered her, and teased her slit and crack, making her squirt on my face when I found that g-spot.

"Okay that's enough...I can't take no more." She crawled into the backseat to get away. Her hair was matted to her sweaty face and her skirt was up to her chest.

I was too cocky, sitting in the front seat, smoking the rest of the blunt from earlier. "You taste like water." I belched and looked at her through the rearview.

"I hate you. You'll have me stalking you like Staci and Angel." She was still shaking and trying

to catch her breath. "Damn you just going to sit there smoking? You know I want that dick now."

I blew smoke at her. "It's up here because if I have to come get it, I promise you're going to regret it."

"I'm not scared of you."

I put the blunt out, then stripped my clothes off. "Take that shit off." I turned the heat on before I got in the backseat.

An hour and a half after we'd originally met, I was watching her Range pull out of the lot of Germantown High, headed home. I fucked her so good that she cried, and at one point, while I had her doggy style, she just buried her face into the seat and shook uncontrollably. I even got her to suck my dick, her first, or so she said. It didn't matter, she swallowed every drop anyway. All in all, she'd been well worth the wait. But she was no Angel, and nowhere close to Staci's freaky ass.

Speaking of Staci, it was her call on my way back to the hood that made me wish I hadn't

turned my phone off. "Baby they had a shootout after the Melrose and Hamilton basketball game. GG was with Lucky, she saw the entire thing. "Hurk and Mo-B had words, then they started shooting at each other."

“What happen?” I asked.

She paused. “Nothing seen, nothing said, but the dudes might not make it."

I smiled. “Baby, I'm on my way over there.”

“N’all, go check on your brothers. You can pick me up from school tomorrow. I love you, and whatever bitch you were with did you a favor, at least you weren't there!”

I laughed. “I love you Staci, good night baby.” I hung up and headed to Hurk’s. He promised to get rid of Mo-B, and if he did, all we had to do now was to make sure he got away with it and we get rid of any other potential threat.

Chapter 17
Icky
"THE OTHER SIDE"

One month later

I pulled into Lucky's driveway and parked my car. He and I were supposed to be going to the mall for some last-minute shopping for our spring break trip to Miami. We were leaving in two days and I still had to get my stuff for the beach.

It had been a few weeks since Hurk got shot and Jinx got arrested. The whole city had been on pins and needles. Aside from the ongoing beef with the Wolfpack, we've been at it with the Pretty Boy Thugs. Just last night, Bounce and Doll Baby got into a fight at a party. It was too crazy and The Dinner Thief Gangsters were directly in the midst of it all.

I got out of my car and went to knock on the door. Lucky's older sister, Maria, answered wearing a pair of tight ass cut off shorts, a white belly shirt, and Jordan's. Her tall ass looked like a damn Kardashian with all that ass sitting up.

"You just gonna stare or are you coming in?" She stepped to the side so I could enter the house.

The smell of kush and fried chicken met me once I was inside. She led the way into the kitchen.

"Lucky had to take GG home, but he should be back in a few minutes." She checked something in the oven. Her shorts rode up, exposing her bare ass and an outline of her fat pussy.

"Anyway, I heard you're a daddy now. You and Lucky started early, I'm surprised Jinx doesn't have three or four already, his sexy ass."

I noted the look in her eyes. She was a *Jewel* too. My lil brah had so many dimes on his team. Shit, he'd fucked Lucky's whole damn family.

"Hello," I answered Bounce's phone call.

"Aye, meet us at *Toya's*. Lucky's on his way up there too."

The doorbell rang and Maria went to answer the door. When she returned, Jinx was holding her hand. He greeted me after I hung up the phone.

"You talk to brah nem?" I asked.

He smacked Maria's ass when she checked the oven. "They called. That fool Buck wants to talk to y'all." He asked Maria to fix him a plate, and then walked me to the door. "Mo-B died this morning," he whispered once we were outside.

"Damn what they say?"

"I don't know. Anyway, I'm finna go in here and handle shawty."

I laughed. "How long you been hitting her?"

He didn't respond, he simply smiled. "I'll be at the spot all night," he said. He showed me love once he walked me to my car.

When I got to *Toya's,* I got out and joined my guys at our usual table. As soon as I sat down, they informed me that our names had come up in the connection with Mo-B's murder investigation. Buck joined us.

"I'll make this short and sweet. You three are costing me a lot of unnecessary favors." He pointed at me, Lucky, and Bounce. "You can't be sloppy, and before you lie to me, let's make this clear, never leave witnesses. Whether it's a senior citizen or damn toddler, if they can talk they can tell on you." He sipped his Corona. "You, walk with me."

The two of us walked out to the parking lot. "Your dad wants you to handle something." He gave me a legal envelope. Inside was my dad's new PSI, Boney and Diego's names were highlighted.

"Diego was found in Cincinnati this morning, he's dead. But if you can't get rid of Boney for Killer D these new charges will get him life."

"I don't know where Boney is." I said.

"He's in Vegas with Cutie Pie. She's expecting you." He gave me a plane ticket. "You should get going, your flight leaves in an hour. I'll call Nyla and let her know you're with me. Don't forget, if they can talk, they can tell," he said with a smile.

Bounce

"CLOSE CALL"

"You sure you don't mind? I know you have to finish packing, I can get Buck to do it."

"Please don't smoke in my car." My sister said, giving me her keys.

"You act like I'm still 15 or 16. I promise not to dog out your 745. I know your baby daddy bought it for you. Shit, I'm only going to get the oil changed and tires rotated."

The door buzzed. "Hold on," Zandria rushed to answer it. "Hi Bad Boy." She sounded like a schoolgirl when she let him in.

"Hi Zion give me some sugar," she said with even more joy.

I gave my nephew and his dad dap on my way out the door. I got in Zandria's car and backed out of the driveway. The Express Oil was only ten minutes from the house, but the traffic on Germantown Parkway made it more like forty-five minutes. I used the extra time to call Valencia and convince her to meet me for ice cream. Naturally, she agreed, and five minutes after I dropped the car off she pulled up.

"You got a dress on?" I asked jokingly. Val was sexy, but she had more of a tomboy style when it came to her clothes. She was the tight jeans, Jordan's type, which made her the perfect choice to be in charge of the female Dinner Thieves. She was a lady though; it was evident by the way she looked when she greeted me with a kiss.

"I had an interview with the scholarship people at the University of Memphis... Anyway, come buy me some chocolate ice cream."

"I got some chocolate for your thin ass." I held the door for her as she entered Baskin Robbins. We placed our orders and then sat on the patio to enjoy ice cream.

"You excited about the trip?" I asked.

"I can't wait. You have Hamilton, Whitehaven, Central, White Station, and Melrose going. With all the enemies and side chicks y'all got. Shit, Jinx and Playa Joe got into it at the mall about an hour ago."

"I thought it was Lucky and Gutter Zed?"

She corrected me, letting me know it was Lucky that defused the altercation, which was over Angel.

"Oh, let's not forget your girl Ebony and her new booh, Ziggy Zaggs."

"I'm eating ice cream with my girl."

"Umm-hmm... Anyway, I still have to buy a bathing suit. Are you coming to the club?"

"Me and Lucky. He's with Kourtney right now."

She read a text. "Damn, this is my brother... I'll see you tonight." I walked her to her Mazda and helped her inside.

By the time I was done with my ice cream and held a fifteen-minute conversation with Lucky, the cats at Express Oil were done with the car. I dropped it off at home, showered, and then drove to South Memphis. I was out of weed, so I stopped by Pasha and Cookie's to fuck off a few dollars with Lil Mane. As usual, he was on the porch with several of the youngsters in the hood. The music was loud, but they were twice as loud.

"What's up big homey." He showed me love as soon as I made it onto the porch. "That's your Infiniti?" he asked.

I smiled proudly. "Yeah, I traded the Cutlass in a few weeks ago. I need an ounce of that good ass weed."

"What's up sucker? Hoe ass nigga, it's Wolfpack. Vice Lord," Super Dave yelled from inside his box Chevy. He threw up gang signs and then flashed a gun before pulling off.

I was strapped too, but I wasn't trying to bring my beef to Pasha and Cookie's spot.

"What's up with him? He must not know what it is?" Lil Mane held his shirt up to reveal his pistol. Several of his youngsters stepped out onto the curb as they were expecting trouble.

Before I could pay for the weed Lil Mane handed me, the car turned the corner and super Dave opened fire. True to the form, my guys and I fired back, causing his car to swerve and hit the curb before he sped into the opposite direction.

I ran out to my car and peeled off. *Bitch ass nigga! I'm g'on kill him,*

I won't have a choice, I said to myself.

Chapter 18
Hurk
"THE PUNISHER"

I woke up to the sound of laughter and the smell of a cake. I took a deep breath after glancing at the alarm clock. It was eight in the damn morning. I normally slept until at least ten on Sunday's but not today.

"Stop ole crazy ass boy!" Angel ran around the kitchen table while Jinx chased her. The two of them had cake mix and icing all over themselves and the kitchen.

"What's up with all this?"

Jinx pulled Angel back into his chest and kissed her lips. It was crazy watching them interact, but it seemed authentic. I mean Jinx had several females, yet Angel's place in his life seemed to surpass any of them, with the exception of Staci, maybe. I had to respect the way he treated my sister though.

"I was baking Amy's birthday cake, but he wanted to play," Angel said.

I tasted the caramel chocolate icing. "Where's everyone?"

"At church." She rolled her eyes when Jinx's phone rang. "I wish you'd tell her to stop calling."

He kissed her, then replied, "She says the same thing about you." He answered, talked for a few seconds, then hung up. "I'll be back in a couple of hours." He gave me dap, and then hurried out to his truck.

"You really like Lil Brah?" I asked, while I watched her clean the mess they'd made.

She was blushing so hard. "I've always liked him but I love him now. And so you'll know, I am not dumb. I know all his business, who he's fucking, how he gets his money, even his secrets. As long as when we're together I feel secure and loved, I'm riding with him. Hell, I'm not ready for him to slow down yet. I need him tired of the fast life when I make him all mine."

"Don't get pregnant," I said before I headed up to my room. I took a shower and got dressed, then I headed to see Buck.

He was on his porch with some Kimbo Slice looking cat when I pulled up. I'd been around Buck for a few months but I'd never seen this dude he was with. He introduced him as Strong Arm, his chief of security.

"Hurk took two bullets a few weeks ago. I took it personal, so I need you to show him a few tricks," Buck said to Strong Arm. "I'm preparing him and his partners for something major and I need him to learn from the best."

Strong Arm smiled, then pointed to the black on black Dodge truck. "You drive."

The two of us left Buck's and went to South Memphis. He directed me to a barbecue joint on Third and Mallory-Interstate.

We got out and went in. "Watch my back," he whispered, then made his way to the kitchen.

"Oh my God!" Someone screamed from the back. I could hear shit breaking before Strong drug some pitiful looking cat out and threw him against the wall.

"Please, tell Bad Boy I'll get the rest of his money." The guy looked terrified. Strong was beating the hell out of him. Every punch was drawing more and more blood. Strong Arm beat him until he couldn't move.

"Get off of him! I'm calling the cops." A lady tried to grab him and he slapped her through a table. He reached inside the man's pocket and took all his cash.

"You hungry?" he turned and asked me. He headed with the guy to the back.

I checked on the lady, but when Strong Arm saw me, he yelled at me. "Leave that bitch alone. Let's go!" He got in the driver's seat.

"You can't have no feelings in this shit. It's a jungle, you got to be a gorilla."

He gave me the bloody money.

"$2500? All that for $2500?" I was insulted.

"It ain't about the money, it's about fear and respect. It'll keep you at the top of the food chain. Never forget that."

Jinx

"MAJOR PAIN"

"Jeremy... I'm glad I caught you. I need a favor."

My mom kissed my cheek and then helped me repack my suitcase for my spring break trip. It had been two or three days since I've seen either of my parents. I had their schedule down to a science, making sure I was only around for breakfast and back by curfew. I loved my folks, but they weren't too pleased with my lifestyle. My mom was cool, but because of how my pops controlled his home, she often stayed out of our disagreements.

"What's up pretty lady? I see you're all dressed to impress looking like a young Lena Horne."

She smiled. For a 45-year-old woman and a mother of two, my mom was still foxy. She retired from the Army seven years ago, but still maintained her physique. She spent most of her free time traveling. My pops, on the other hand, was still in full-time soldier mode.

"I want you and Jamie to come to dinner with Major Vaughn and I."

"Tonight I'm taking Angel to the movies since I'm leaving in the morning."

She smiled. "Angel? Hurk's sister? What happened to Miss Staci, I thought you two were pretty serious?"

"We are, but so is Angel and me. Anyway, you should've let me know ahead of time."

"You're never here." She helped me zip the suitcase. "It's only a dinner. As a matter of fact, invite Angel too."

Before I could agree, my dad walked into my room.

"Let's go," he said.

"I was just telling Jeremy to invite his girlfriend."

"For what?"

"Cause I had plans tonight that I'm canceling."

He laughed. "Good, then let's go. You can take that girl out another time."

"Mane, you trippin'," I replied.

"Jeremy… Major, let him."

He cut her off. "Shut up Nina. I am sick of this ungrateful, selfish son of ours. He's an embarrassment."

"You act like I'm proud to be yours. Nigga you ain't winning no damn father of year awards."

My mom stepped in between the two of us. "Stop it!"

"N'all ma... I'm tired of him always criticizing me like he's Cliff Huxtable. This is why I'm never here, because of him."

Whop!

He punched me in my mouth. Without thinking, I hit him with a two piece to the face. We fought until my mom and my sister pulled us apart.

"Get out!" he blurted, wiping the blood from his mouth. "You are dead to me!"

"I'm sorry Ma, but he's wanted to say that for too long." I held my head up and looked him square in the eyes. "You thought it would be easy... this ain't that."

"You have 15 minutes, after that I'm not responsible." He turned and limped away.

"What happen?" My sister asked. My mom hugged me and told me not to leave, that she'd talked to Major Vaughn. Jamie looked at the cut on my hand.

"You actually fought him? You're lucky he didn't kill you."

"I'm not scared to die." I lifted my shirt so she could see I had a pistol on me the entire time. "Anyway, help me take my clothes to the truck. I don't want shit he bought, just my clothes and shit. Let Ma know I'll call her when I get to Miami."

It only took ten minutes to get my stuff. All I took were my clothes, jewelry, shoes, and my PlayStation 3. When I left, I went by Staci's. I had to drop off some money so she could pick up some last minute things for our trip. She couldn't believe I fought Major Vaughn. She talked to my mom before I got there, promising she'd try to talk me into going home.

Needless to say, I wasn't at Staci's too long.

I left there and went to get Angel. Hurk and Xaviera were in the driveway when I pulled up. "You're a little over packed for five nights and six days." Hurk noticed all the clothes on the backseat.

"It's a long story. Anyway, where's Angel?"

"In the house."

I went in and straight up to Angel's room. She was doing her hair, singing Keyshia Cole's *Love.* I put my arms around her and kissed her shoulder.

"You in love now?"

"I've been in love booh." She put the curlers down and turned to face me. "What bitch burst your lip and got your face all scratched up?"

"Me and Major Vaughn got into a fight. Anyway, how much longer you need?" I opened her robe and took a good look at her. She had on a pair of pink lace boy shorts and a matching bra.

"I'm almost ready."

"Damn Angel, you getting thick. Hips and ass spreading, little titties growing. Who you fucking?"

She blushed and tried to cover herself. "Stop, I'm trying to get dressed."

"Fuck that, I wanna go under." I closed the bathroom door. "Where is your mom?"

She let me sit her on the counter. "She took Amy to the circus, Alicia and Alexis are at the Grizzilies' game."

"Perfect. Can I do me?"

"You got a rubber because I'm out of birth control until this Wednesday."

"Fuck all that. This pussy is mine. Now shut up so I can make you scream."

Chapter 19
Lucky
"WARNING SHOTS"

Spring Break

"Hey Lorenzo. Dang, we ain't on speaking terms," Hannah Dunn rolled her eyes at me as she walked by. Hannah was my ex-girlfriend, a senior at Melrose. She and I dated in the ninth grade and broke up when I hooked up with Iysis. She was sexy, tall, and model like, but far too ratchet for me. I was posted with my guys when she passed. We were all at the airport awaiting our flight to Miami. There were close to 800 students and teachers from five different high schools, all headed for five days of fun in the sun. I was not trying to start with crazy ass Hannah Dunn and her burgundy and gold weave.

"What's up Hannah?" I gave a nonchalant head nod, choosing to play it cool.

She walked over and stood in front of me. "What's up? Oh so now it's what's up?"

"Don't try to shine on brah because he ain't trying to entertain your big head ass. The way the whole Orange Mound done ran thru your beat up ass pussy, his dick probably did feel little." Jinx laughed at his own humor.

"I don't care about you gettin' mad go tell your weak ass nigga what I said," he added.

The five of us walked away, headed towards our flight terminal.

"This is going to be a crazy ass trip," I said. "You got *PMP. The*

Showstoppers Dimes and Divas, *Eye Candy*, *Gettin'Money Clique*, *PBT*, and the pussy ass *Wolfpack*." I spotted one of my old chicks. "Oh shit, y'all see Kima."

Jinx laughed. "I don't want no old ass pussy. I'm avoiding Staci as much as I can."

"You need to leave your phone. Angel's going to call and text you the whole trip." Hurk punched Jinx in the chest.

Bounce pointed towards a group of females "They goin'?" he asked. "Damn, real snow bunnies."

We posted near Starbucks and watched the females as they went inside. "Here comes trouble." I spotted Murder Mook and Yinka as they walked our way.

"What up?" Yinka mean mugged Jinx.

"Quit stuntin', you know what it is." Jinx smiled at them and said, "keep playin', you g'on be next on First 48. Thinkin' it's a game."

Vida stepped between us. Her and the dude Yinka were messing around, even though she was *D.T.G.* They walked away wisely before things got ugly.

"I'm sick of them," Hurk growled. He had a scary look on his face, like he was ready to kill on sight. He'd been that way since he got shot.

Tia Pham and Staci walked over. Staci claimed Jinx's full attention, while Tia asked to speak with me in private. She and I stepped away from the crowd. She seemed nervous. I mean, I knew she had a crush on me. Hell, I felt the same way. Who wouldn't like Tia. She was cute and she was a genius too.

"Quit being shy," I said with a smile. She turned two shades redder when I touched her face.

"I was wondering if you'd trade seats with Staci, maybe you and I can get to know each other," she said.

"That's cool if you think you can handle being that close to me."

She played with my Boston Celtics chain and smiled. "Should I unpack my blanket?"

"You think you'll need it?"

"Maybe... I mean, there's no telling what you'll try or what I might let you get into."

I noticed a small crowd forming near Jinx and Staci. "I'll meet you on the plane." I kissed her cheek, and then hurried towards the crowd.

"Hoe, I know you set me up! All hugged up with this bitch!" Ziggy Zaggs pointed his finger in Jinx's face, but was talking to Staci.

Jinx held Staci and kissed her face. "You g'on get your chance homey. I go all over the city, you know how to find me."

Coach Hill and Coach Tate stepped between Jinx and Ziggy Zaggs. "Listen up, anymore

altercations or incidents and this trip is canceled... You understand?" Coach Hill looked at us.

"Do you understand?" Coach Tate repeated. We all nodded our heads yes.

I pulled Jinx to the side. "Brah, chill out we'll handle all oppositions when we get back."

Icky

"Slip, Never Fall"

"I'm telling y'all, all we have to do is keep a low profile while we're here, Buck took care of everything," Lucky said.

I stepped onto the balcony and lit a joint. Bounce joined me.

"Who are you in the room with?" he asked.

"Trevor Miller, Youngblood, and Sandman. I'm not sleeping until I get back on the plane. It's too many hoes down here. Nyla is too."

Jinx took a couple of pictures of the city from our 19th floor balcony. "We have two things to plan around, the 7 o'clock count at breakfast and the midnight curfew."

"Fuck all that, I'm trying to fuck a model or video hoe." Lucky joined us.

"We got tickets to the Miami and New York game tomorrow night." I showed them the tickets. "I told you, Buck fucks with us."

Knock! Knock!

Ms. Cunningham walked into the room. I dropped the joint over the balcony and held in

the smoke. She came all the way to the balcony door. "I need to talk to you four and to you too Ike Turner." She pinched my nostrils closed. "Please, don't make us regret this trip. I know you're young and very popular, but please try to respect the rules."

from her direction.

"Curfew is at 11p.m.," she told us.

"This say midnight." I showed her the itinerary.

"You have to be inside your rooms by midnight. I'll be personally checking this floor and don't try me." She smiled before she left.

Jinx lit a blunt. "I believe I can fuck her old ass." We all laughed continuing to get high until it was time to leave.

It was slightly after 4 p.m. when Lucky, Hurk, Bounce, and I went to check out Buck's condo. The place was plush. Five minutes from the beach, marble flooring, and it was fully stocked too. We had clothes in our sizes, Buck's drop-top 745 and his Range, not to mention the weed and alcohol.

I called to thank him.

“I was just about to call you,” he answered. “That job was impressive. Come see me when you get home.”

“I will. Anyway, thank you for the set up.”

He laughed. “It's nothing. Make sure you make lifelong memories and stay out of trouble.”

I hung up and smiled. My heart was heavy, but relieved. I killed my Uncle Boney, but I may have saved my dad's life. I was just glad I’d gotten away with murder again, which was exactly why I was going to enjoy and remember every moment of this trip.

Chapter 20

Bounce

"THE UNDERSTANDING"

The beauty of South Beach brought a smile to my face. I sat on the trunk of the blue drop top, my Carolina blue Jordan's set matched the paint perfectly. All eyes were on us, as they should've been.

"Hi Kevion," Bridgett York spoke to me as she walked by. Her and her girls were known as *The Showstoppers,* each went to White Station High, and Bridgett was the only white chick. She was a sexy blonde with big breasts and long legs. She and I had been friends all our lives because our parents were good friends.

"What's up? You workin' that two-piece." I got up and gave her a hug. She moved a few strands of her wavy blonde hair, and then asked whose car I was on. I told her it was Zandria's baby daddy's. She looked around and to my surprise, she asked where Valencia was.

"She went with her friends to the mall. Where's T. Speed?"

"Boy please, he is not my type," she replied. We continued to flirt, even when Birdie and Smurf snatched Lucky's shorts down and exposed his naked ass.

"Aye... heads up," Icky said. I watched Jinx as he went to cut Staci and Ebony off. They were headed directly towards us too.

"If you can get Jinx to sneak off with you, we'd love to keep you guys company." Bridgett walked back to where her girls were.

Ebony rolled her eyes at Bridgett. "Blue eyed skank."

"That's exactly why don't nobody want you except Gangster Greg. Fine as you are, you're too insecure," Jinx said.

"Fuck you punk. That's why you're homeless!" she shot back.

"Girl come on before you get him started." Staci pulled Ebony and headed back towards the hotel. "7:15 Jeremy, don't make me call you."

Jinx smiled as soon Staci walked off he said, "C'mon, we got two hours to play. I'm finna put Mercedes and Teresa down, and Bridgett wants you to come too."

"Where they going?" I watched Lucky, Icky, and Hurk leave in the Range.

"I didn't ask. C'mon, it's 5 o'clock." Jinx got in the car and tossed me the keys. "Let's go fool."

When we got to the condo, all the guys were there and the three females were just pulling up. Jinx lit a few blunts, Lucky popped a few bottles, while Hurk hooked up the video camera. Every girl we put down was getting put on tape.

"This ain't Girls Gone Wild!" Mercedes said. She was the head cheerleader at White Station, the leader of *The Showstoppers*. Mercedes Good had been in love with Jinx for as long as she'd known him, but was too stingy to share him.

Jinx got up and started to dance on her. One thing about lil brah, he was a cold gangster, but the boy could move like Omarion! Mercedes tried not to blush, but she couldn't help it. She pulled Theresa up and they sandwiched him. Teresa was his ex-booh, the one Dominique took him from. She was bad too, like a thick half-Black, half-Colombian and a real good girl until she met Jinx.

"Aye brah, we gotta roll," Hurk told me.

"Go where?" I asked out of frustration. When I noticed he had on all black, I remembered the job Buck had for us. We were supposed to break into Vago's South Beach home!

Jinx looked at us. "We are you going?"

"Something came up. Make sure you tape it." I kissed Bridgett. "I'll make it up to you," I promised.

I rushed out to the Range and got in. "Let's go get this paper. Shit, I hope it's worth it, I just turned down some exclusive pussy."

"I'll buy you some before we leave," Lucky said with a smile as he pulled off.

Hurk

"STACKS ON DECK"

"Look fool... 3 on 1, and they still couldn't hang! I had so much of this rod in Mercedes, she was crying big tears. I fucked Teresa to sleep, and Bridgett let me go in her ass!" Jinx bragged while we watched the footage from the tape he'd made with *The Showstoppers*.

"Damn... I love you brah, but I can't fuck no hoe with you or after your nasty ass." Icky gave him dap and laughed.

I passed Bounce the blunt. "You did shine. You don't be on my little sister like that?" I asked Jinx.

"Shit'd...why not? Anyway, I need to text my shawty and make sure she's cool." He pulled his phone out and started to type.

"How you get rid of Staci?" I asked Jinx after checking to see what all the commotion outside our room was about.

"I ate her pussy and her ass til she squirted in my mouth... Then I gave her what I had left."

"Noooo... Lucky, what's wrong with him!" Bounce said.

"Why you askin', Lucky? He's been a butt muncher since he fucked Iysis."

"You must've forgotten I saw the tape you made with Cookie and Pasha?" Lucky said to me.

I laughed. "Fuck all that, it's only 9:45. What we finna do? I parked the truck on the beach."

Lucky and Icky counted the money from their pockets. I knew they were anxious to spend some of the cash we had taken when we jacked the

Mexicans a few hours prior. "Let's roll," they said in unison.

Lucky grabbed the keys to the BMW, but Jinx's crazy ass said he was chilling. He was on the phone with Angel. We snuck out of the hotel by taking the stairs, then running out the fire exit. We decided to go to the King of Diamonds. Buck knew the cat that owned it so we had no trouble getting in.

"Look fool... It's Rick Ross and Trina." Lucky saluted them as we made our way by their table. "That nigga built like a silverback!" Bounce said. Icky was too busy counting money.

"You wanna stunt? It's free money, you know my motto." I pulled out several stacks and put them on the table.

"Shit, I forgot about this $20,000. This from Boney's rat ass!" Icky snapped. "Dinner Thieves in this bi-otch!"

Bounce and Lucky's smiled, both signaling for a lap dance.

"What's up sexy? Put that ass in my lap." Lucky put several hundred dollars in her g- string. The mamacita sat in his lap, the snow bunny did the same to Bounce.

I ordered the drinks. "Send the table of females two bottles of Rose and tell them their night is on us. Keep the change," I told our server. "We want bottles of the best champagne and send Ross and Trina one. Tell them *The Dinner Thieves* appreciate the southern hospitality," I said as he gave the waitress way too much money.

"Where y'all from?"

"Memphis!" we all replied.

"*Dinner Thief Gangsters*! Matter of fact, tell the DJ to play some YoGotti... Juicy J... Hell, he can play some 8-Ball-n-MJG, just make us feel at home," Icky added.

"Never get full my nigga. Snatch plates, but never get full," I saluted his cockiness, feeling the same way! After this trip, nothing about our lives would ever be the same.

Chapter 21

Jinx

"QUALITY TIME"

"Have you decided what you're going to do when you get home? I mean, at least where you going to live?" I put my arm around Staci as we continued to walk down the sandy beach. We'd been in Miami for a couple of days now, but this was the first time that the two of us had been alone long enough to talk about us. We've been on the beach since 8 a.m. and it was now 10:30.

"Jeremy, are you listening to me?" She pinched me to reclaim my attention.

I kissed her nose. "I was thinking. I'll probably get a spot by myself, but in Jamie's name." I stopped and pulled her into my arms. "You still plan on going to UT-Knoxville?"

"Either there or Spelman, whoever pays the most scholarship money. Why? You nervous about a long-distance relationship?"

I looked into her gray eyes and it hit me I was in love with Staci! I mean, I still had other girls and I was feeling Angel, but Staci was the crème of the crop. She had super model looks and sex appeal; she was smart, funny, supportive, understanding, and independent enough to stand on her own. Maybe that's what scared me, the fact that she didn't need me the way the others did.

"Honestly I think I'm a little nervous. You know how I feel about you."

"You still can't say it." She smiled.

"I love you."

She cried as if she'd waited a lifetime to hear those words. I was only being honest though. I mean, I showed it daily, but it was the first time I'd spoken those words.

My phone ruined our moment. I answered, but only because I thought it was Vago and I-40. Someone robbed one of their stash spots, killed several of their workers, and stole over half a mil in cash and product.

"What's up booh? What are you doing?" Angel asked.

"I'm talking to Staci. Can I call you back?"

"No. Fuck that mutt...fake ass creole... Tell her to go wax her sideburns and her stomach."

I couldn't help but laugh. "Bye."

"Don't you hang up. I need to tell you something."

I pulled Staci back to my chest when she attempted to walk away. "What is it?" I asked Angel.

"I'm pregnant."

My stomach dropped into my shoes. "Are you serious?"

"Eight weeks. I found out thirty minutes ago. Anyway, I love you, now tell your girlfriend her days are numbered." She hung up.

"Hmp... Who was that? Angel, Mercedes, Tameka, or Yasmin." Staci asked.

"That was Jamie trying to get me to call Major Vaughn. My mom went to Chicago after I left." I lied about my phone call, but the rest of it was true.

"You should at least consider it. I mean, at least your dad gives you some kind of attention. I live with mine and the only time he's around is when he's giving me my allowance, or when he has to pretend we're a happy family."

"I keep forgetting your dad is the big shot political cat." I laughed.

"Whatever... You'd better enjoy your freedom because when we have our child, I'm locking you down."

"You pregnant?" I asked.

She punched my chest.

"I want you, but aren't I worth a ring and a home first? At least a new car."

"Quit hitting on me. I just told you I love you." I kissed her, relieved to know she wasn't pregnant.

"What if I want one though?" I asked. She walked a few steps in front of me, then stopped and looked at me.

"Promise me regardless of what happens with us, you'll always keep a spot in your heart for me." She held my hands and continued. "I want to be a physician, that's not a career for a teenage mom, and school is too important for me to put my life on hold to become a wife. I love you more than enough to wait, but this monster is in your linen shorts has a mind of its own.

Just don't make me regret pursuing a dream I had before I met you." She kissed my mouth and smiled like she was up to no good.

"What?" I asked.

"I want some dick before I let you run off with your boys, before Mercedes calls."

"What's up with this Mercedes shit?"

She laughed. "Boy please, don't act like you aren't trying to fuck her pretty black ass. You better let her know, I'll beat her ass the same way I did Vida, Star, and Cookie."

Once we left the beach, the two of us spent the next four hours in her room. We agreed to spend the night together, but that we should hang with our friends until then.

I went back to my room, showered, and got dressed for the night.

"Aye Jinx, why you ain't dressed for the game?" Icky asked. He walked in rocking an exclusive D-Wade jersey with two rose gold chains on. When he smiled, I noticed he finally made good on his promise, he had 32 rose gold teeth and some had rubies in them.

I shook my head and smiled. "I'm chilling tonight."

"That fool in love," Lucky replied. "Damn shame, all that good pussy and he can't get over Staci."

I went to answer the door, it was Mercedes. "Hi fellas," she said as she stepped inside.

"Shit... girl where your waist at? Them khaki shorts fittin' like skin," Lucky said as he eyeballed her flawless frame.

"Where y'all headed?" Bounce asked.

"It's a secret." Mercedes pulled me into the hallway and down to the elevators. We were getting on when Ziggy and Yellow Boy got off with Vida, Birdie, and Smurf. He smiled. I knew he'd tell Staci.

“What up gangster?” Smurf showed me love, her little ass looked at Mercedes, then at me.

“You got some kush?” she asked. Vida and Ziggy kept walking.

“You can speak Mercedes,” Birdie smiled and said.

“What's up y’all. Anyway, come on Jeremy I'm starving.”

I gave Smurf the bag of kush I had.

“Nothing seen, nothing said,” I whispered.

“Boy please, I ain't no rat. Just make sure you don't eat too much of that chocolate.”

I got onto the elevator and smiled. “You so full of shit,” I told Mercedes.

“No I'm not I'm just trying to steal Staci Armstrong's man, the same way she did to Dominique Ellis, and I plan on being your top priority too. So all your side hoes might as well get ready.”

“We'll see. We will see.”

Part Two

Chapter 1
Lucky
"LOOSE CANNON"

One Year Later

"Lucky, are you still taking me and Latrell to the doctor tomorrow?" Iysis sat her bubble butt in my lap and twisted my little afro.

"Yeah, at 9:15. Did you call and set up a time for us to take pictures?"

She got up and picked our son up from the couch. "We go on Friday afternoon. I want to go shopping though. We'll go tomorrow when we leave the doctor." I kissed both her and our son. "I'll call you tonight."

She walked me to the door. "Are you still going to the club?"

"For a little while. You know what, I'm spending the night with y'all. Go take a nap."

I got in my brand-new triple black Corvette and pulled out of Iysis' driveway. In the past year, so much in my life changed. Not only was the Vette brand-new, but I had a six-month-old son by Iysis named Latrell, and a seven-month-old son by Courtney named Lorenzo Jr. Junior was born September 11, Trell was born October 9. But neither one of them was my girl. That title belonged to Tia Pham!

I also had a new hustle. After my guys and I pulled off that big lick for Buck in Miami, I was able to start my own modeling company. With Jinx as a partner, *The Bad Luck Girls* quickly became the hottest thing in urban modeling!

In 9 months, we'd placed girls in videos, commercials, fashion shows, low-budget films, and several urban magazines.

Tonight we were sponsoring a contest at Buck's new club. The winner was to receive five thousand in cash and a seven page spread in Straight Stuntin' magazine.

Since it was Sunday, instead of hoe hopping, I decided to spend some quality time with Tia. After she and I hooked up in Miami, we decided to keep it going. She was in school at the University of Memphis, as a criminal justice major. Since we started dating I found out a huge secret, Tia was bisexual and a cold nympho too!

When I got to her apartment she was washing my money green S550. Her lil body looked good in daisy dukes and a damp wife beater.

"Why are you out here washing my car? I got junkies in the hood that need to work." I kissed her mouth.

"I don't mind, plus Erin was helping. You look handsome." She admired my blue and purple Coogi set. I smacked her booty and told her how sexy she looked.

"What's up Lorenzo," Erin spoke when she stepped off the porch. She too had on daisy dukes and a wife beater, and like Tia her hair was in a braided ponytail. Tia pulled me inside with Erin shutting the door once we were in the den. Tia mentioned the weed I left, Erin offered to fix me a drink.

I sat on the couch and dialed Jinx's number. Angel answered and let me know he was asleep. She also informed me that he'd meet me at *Bad Boys* by 10 p.m. By the time I hung up, Erin had fixed me a lemonade and Ciroc. Tia gave me the ounce of dro, and then said something to Erin about taking a quick shower.

"I heard you and Jeremy on the radio today." Erin licked and sucked the cigar before she split it and dumped the tobacco into the ashtray.

My dick jumped, not only from watching her handle the cigar, but I could see her fat vagina while she sat on the floor.

"Why you not in the contest?" I asked while rolling the blunt.

"I'm too shy," she replied with a smile.

I lit the blunt. "You weren't shy the other day when you were diggin' in that lil juice box. I saw you watchin' me fuck your roommate. That dick looked good to you?"

"Whatever."

"You wanted some? You want it right now?" I said as I passed her the weed. "Tia told me y'all been suckin' pussy, I wanna see... Shit, I wanna suck it too."

She sat blushing, with her thighs were wide open. "What about Tia."

"Oh, that's my booh, she knows what's up. Now, put that blunt out and go get in the shower."

"I'm not."

I stripped my clothes off and stood up. "Yes, you are. Now, c'mon before I call Tia and make her hold you down. Playin' with me like my name ain't Lucky Mendes."

Jinx

"THE CHOSEN"

"Brah, Where are you?"

"I am in the hood. Why, what's up?" I asked Lucky. I could hear the loud music in the background so I knew he was at the club. I also knew he expected me to be there, but I had money to make. Plus, it was going down at Lil Mane's, him and my little soldiers were having a house party.

"The contest brah...You're a judge," Lucky said. I laughed at the fight that had just broken out. Lil Mane and two brothers were putting down a new recruit. "I pick Staci...or Angel...or Mercedes."

"So you're not coming?" Lucky replied.

"I'll be there. I gotta go brah." I hung up and punched the new brother so hard he fell in the middle of the street. Several other brothers helped him up, all showing him love as they did.

"C'mon, let's get you cleaned up," Val said to him. "Never get full lil brah." I gave him a roll of cash and a bag of weed after he and I shook hands. "Aye Tierra, go show the lil brother some love"

"That boy ain't but 'bout 13," she replied.

I laughed at the way she rolled her eyes at me. "He got to learn one day." My phone rang. "Yeah."

"May I speak to Jeremy?"

"Who is this?" I answered.

"Damn, now you don't know my voice."

I showed the homies some love, then let Lil Mane know I was out.

"What's up Miss Davis?" I flirted with August.

"Where are you?"

"Wherever you need me to be." I pulled off the block and headed to meet August. I let her know I was in South Memphis, she was in Cordova, at one of her friend's house. She called me to get some weed, but I was anticipating another night like our last one.

It took almost an hour for me to get to London's home. August was on the porch waiting for me when I pulled up in my new burnt orange Lexus GS 400. I could see the lust in her eyes. Plus, I was wearing a fresh ass exclusive pair of orange and tan suede Jordan's, baggy tan khaki shorts and a white T-shirt, with a big ass Glock 40 on my hip, the epitome of dope boy fresh, ya dig!

"Turn your music down," she whispered. I had that Gucci Mane and Yo Gotti up so loud that dogs were barking! I turned the car off.

"My fault whose car are you in?" she asked.

I sat on the trunk and sparked a blunt. "This is my car. I bought it yesterday. Anyway, come give me a hug, got me way out here. Ain't no streetlights. They're still hanging niggas out here."

She laughed as she hugged me. "I figured you were at the club."

"Ain't no money in the club. Shit, I gotta make up what I spent on this car. Plus, I saw a Cadillac I want too."

London walked out of the house and down to where we were. I'd met her before, her and August were best friends. She was stuck up and judging from the type of neighborhood she lived in, I understood why. "Y'all dressed alike?"

London rolled her eyes. "We had to cheer tonight, of course we are dressed alike."

"Stop it," August told her.

I passed her the blunt. "I forgot, you two are big time college girls now. Why aren't you two at the club or one of those frat parties."

"Because, we wanted to hang out with you." August took my rose gold chain off my neck and put it around her own.

"Speak for yourself," London added. Her mouth was saying one thing, but I could tell from the look in her eyes that she was intrigued by my persona.

"Anyway, you want to come in?"

I checked the text from Lucky- he asked if I was coming to the club.

"Y'all ain't going to get me in there and rape me? Your evil ass ain't had no dick in a while, and I don't trust you," I said to August. She laughed at what I said about London.

“You are wrong.”

“Well, I'm not lying.”

“You disrespectful dog. Fuck you Jeremy.” London hit me in my stomach.

I laughed. “Suck my dick,” I replied.

“You wish... Lil dick bastard.”

I stood up and pulled my pants down to my ankles. I wasn't ashamed of the 9 inches I was blessed with!

“I can't stand you.” She turned and walked off, still cursing and mumbling while she did.

August was laughing so hard tears rolled from her eyes. “You are crazy. Now I'll have to hear her all night.”

I fixed my shorts. “Not if you leave with me. I'll listen to you scream my name.”

“Mmm… I can't, we have to be at school in the morning for practice. The NCAA tournament starts next week, but if you go talk to her, I'm sure you can stay here long enough for me to get what I want.” She put her hand in my shorts and squeezed my rod.

“What about your sidekick?” She had a devious look on her face as she pulled me up to the house. Once inside she led me to London's bedroom.

“Get out!” London was just stepping out of her clothes, about to get inside the shower. August kissed her lips forcefully, and then squeezed her breasts until she submitted.

“He wants to say he's sorry. Don't you?”

“I'm too gangster for that sorry shit, but I do want to make it up to you.”

London bit her bottom lip while August fingered her clit. “Kiss my ass,” she said to me.

“I'm with that too.” I smiled while they undressed me. “I just want y’all to know, it ain't shit nice about what's about to go down. I'm high, I'm missing money, and I feel like y’all set me up. So I have to be 100% gangster about giving out this dick.”

“That's all we ask now please, stop talking and put us down!”

Chapter 2

Icky

"NOBODY CROSSES ME"

"Where you been all day? Damn, your side bitch got you scared to answer your phone?"

"Aye Nyla, I ain't got time for that shit. I'll be home when I leave the studio."

I hung up, then turned the music back up. I was listening to the track I'd just rapped on. Over the past year I'd done so much grimy shit in the streets, I decided to start rapping about it. Buck owned a studio, and it had become my second home. I formed a group with Yellow Boy, my cousin Trevor, and Val's brother, Youngblood.

Trevor added some sound effects to the track. "Aye Slick, we need to put a female on the hook." He did a line of coke. "Speaking of females, I fucked Sheena Harris after the contest Sunday night."

"Pretty Tony might blow your ass off about that hoe," I replied.

He laughed and said, "He's too busy chasing Dominique. That girl went to college and came back super bad! She fucking with Duck," Yellow Boy added.

I did a line of coke. "That bitch can't stand me. She still thinks I told Jinx she fucked Buck. I knew, but I ain't said shit. I'm not saying shit and y'all ain't either."

Youngblood added his two cents. "Brah ain't worried, he got ole sexy ass Staci. She's flyin' back to Memphis every other weekend for damn fool!"

"Yeah, Plus, I saw that boy at the movies last night with Buck's daughter," Yellow Boy said.

I did another line of coke, and then popped a 4-bar. "Old- school g'on kill Jinx bout his daughter. Ain't no tellin' what lil brah doin' to her Lauren London lookin' ass. That fool lickin' booty, toes, pussy. He too nasty. If he gets your bitch, she ain't yours anymore,"

I laughed. "Speaking of which, I'm out." I got my keys and headed out the studio.

My Crown Vic sounded like two mad pit bulls! I turned my music up as loud as it would go, then

popped our demo in. The day was beautiful. I was Gucci from my shades to my sneakers, and I was feeling good! I was feeling so good that I changed my mind about going home to Nyla, and decide to go see Star.

"Hey Slick." She wrapped her arms around me and kissed my lips as soon as I stepped inside of her apartment. The first thing I noticed was the strawberry fragrance she wore.

"You smell good... You look good too," I complimented her white pencil skirt and teal blouse.

She let me know she'd been at work; she was a secretary at a law firm. The two of us had been getting closer and closer, especially since Nyla and I had been having problems.

"Terio dropped that money off at my job." She gave me the cash. "I saw some rims I wanted they were $2600, but I got them for $1600."

I laughed, knowing she'd sucked or fucked $1000 off.

"When do you pick um up?"

She undid my jeans and pulled my wood out. "Boy please, they got put on while I was there... Oh, I went ahead and paid your truck note too."

I kissed her nose. "You know I love you... So damn bossy. I wish my punk ass baby momma was more like you... Ever since she had Koby she's been on some dumb shit." My phone vibrated.

"Yeah," I answered.

"This Gangsta, you straight?"

"Yeah, I'm in the Mound, at Star's."

"I'll be there in fifteen minutes." He hung up.

I pinned Star on her back, pushed her skirt over her waist and went in her raw. I hated two things, panties and condoms- Star felt the same way! I spent the next 10 minutes digging into her guts. I was in the bathroom washing up when I heard the dogs barking on the side of the apartment. I grabbed my Desert Eagle and stepped out of the door.

Boow! Boow! Boow! Boow! Boow!

I fired at the masked man that was about to kick the door in. His partners fired at me as they fled the scene.

"Stupid Mu'fucker!" I cursed after removing the dead man's mask it was Super Dave

Jinx

"STREETS AIN'T SAFE"

"That fool merked Super Dave and he shot another dude... He's at the house with Nyla and Koby. I called Ebony and asked her to check on Star, but Gangster Greg already went and got her... Anyway, I gotta go, your sister is jealous."

Hurk laughed. "A'ight lil brah."

I hung up and rested my head in Angel's lap. She put our baby girl on my chest, and plucked a few loose eyebrows from my face.

"You okay?" she asked after a couple of minutes.

"Yeah, just hoping Icky's bullshit won't start a war... Brah 'nem been doing a lot of sneaky shit."

She checked Angelica's diaper, and then picked her up so she could change her.

"What time are you meeting I-40?"

I checked my watch. "In 45 minutes. You're so damn nosey." I smacked her ass, and then put my Jordan's on. "I'll be back after I leave the spot."

"Wake me up when you get here." She kissed me and then held Angelica up so I could kiss her too. "We love you, be careful."

I left my spot in Castalia and went to meet my connect. As I drove I had time to reflect. In a year, I managed to get my life in order- my own home, I brand-new Lexus, I had money in the bank, and a beautiful baby girl. I also had half ownership in *The Bad Luck Girls*. Plus, twenty percent of *Dinner Thief Records*.

I was doing well, so I knew I'd eventually take a loss. That's not what had me worried, it was the shit my guys had going with Buck that I wasn't comfortable with. I picked up the 25 birds from I-40 and took them straight to my stash spot. I'd sit on them a day or two before I got on my grind.

I was on my way home when I got a call from Ebony. She just got back from the Sean John fashion show in New York and wanted me to take her to dinner and a movie. Ebony was the top earner at our agency. I couldn't let her down.

When I got to her townhouse I called to let her know I was out front. While I waited, I put on a Trey Songz album and put in a DVD from Icky's last show. A smile spread across my face as I watched Ebony make her way to the car. She had on a sexy red halter dress and stiletto heels. Shawty was Beyoncé sexy.

"Put on your red dress," I said and I did my best Johnny Gill impression.

She laughed. "You like it? I got it from the fashion show. I love your lil orange and gray polo set, lil orange Maury sandals."

"Where you want to eat?" I asked as I pulled out of her complex.

"Sonic! I'm dying for a chili cheese coney and some fries... Oh, and hot fudge sundae."

I laughed at how excited she seemed.

"I thought you wanted to go out."

"This is out." She laughed too. "I haven't had Sonic in over a year. Besides, I'm not trying to share you tonight. I'm surprised you weren't busy when I called."

"Put this in for me." She took the "Love Jones" DVD from out of my case and handed to me.

I pointed to the button and told her how to remove the DVD inside the player. My phone played Beyoncé's *Ego*. It was Staci calling.

"What's up Miss Armstrong."

"Dang, what happened to hey my shorty?" she whined. "You must be with one of your little chicken heads?"

"Cut it out. Anyway, hey my shorty. What's up?"

"I miss you. I can't wait until next weekend. Can't you drive up here tomorrow night and stay until Sunday?"

I thought for a second. "I can do that. Make sure you let them lil dudes know I got plenty of what they like. And I want you to plan something special for us."

"Okay, thank you Jeremy, I love you so much."

"I love you too, Staci. I'll call you when I leave the city tomorrow."

"That's so sweet. You going to see your booh," Ebony teased me after I hung up.

I laughed. "That's why I can do what I do."

"You just haven't met your match. Staci is cool though, it's Mercedes I can't stand." She gagged. "Her gold diggin' ass!"

"Fuck that... What's up with you and Bounce?"

She rolled her eyes at me. "He's too sprung on Val for me to keep chasing him... Plus, I need a man that's not insecure or afraid to put me in my place. And I like to be fucked like a big girl. Get mad and beat this pussy every now and then." The two of us laughed at her last statement.

"Anyway, I saw Angel and Angelica. That baby is too pretty!"

"I know, she spoiled already." I had a proud smile on my face just talking about my daughter.

"I can smell what I want," she said as soon as I turned into Sonic's lot.

"You put that dress on to come here?"

She rubbed my face and purred. "I wore the dress to impress you. I wanted to come here so the whole city wouldn't be in our business. Bounce is your boy, Staci is my girl, and I work for you. But, one day soon, none of that will matter. For now, I want you all to myself."

"What you trying to tell me?"

She leaned over and kissed my mouth, letting her hand grip my crotch.

"I know what I want. The type of man you are and I trust that you can bring out the best in me."

I reached inside the console and gave her the necklace I bought for her. "This is for all your success."

"It's beautiful. Ooh and these diamonds are so blue and clear. They're real."

"You may be a *Bad Luck Girl*, but I consider you a *Jewel*. My jewel. But I need you to respect the part of my life that does not involve you, and in return I'll keep that smile on your face."

She kissed me again, this time slipping her tongue into my mouth.

"Okay... I promise. Now, can we order because I'm starving."

"Push that damn button. I'm having what you are."

Chapter 3
Bounce
"JEALOUSY"

One month later

"You been on some funny shit. If you're fucking somebody else just keep it real. It has to be another nigga somewhere long as I've been knowing you I never fucked you in your ass, and you never swallowed my seeds. Now you're begging for that shit!"

Ebony pushed me out of her way and walked out of my bedroom. "That's your problem! You can't handle me because you're too insecure and when was the last time we went out together?"

I thought for a few seconds. "We went to the club last weekend."

"No, you were there when I got there you, left with Bridgett. I went home alone." "You're always busy. You were in New York for two weeks."

She continued to pack her things. "I invited you. Look, we just. I have someone. I can't keep doing this with you."

"Bitch, quit playin' with me."

"Let my arm go!" She snatched away from me, and then slapped me.

Whop!

I backhanded her and then kicked her while she was on the floor.

"Fuck you think I am!" I taunted her.

"I hate you!" She ran to her purse and pulled her pistol out. "Get back!"

There was a knock at the door before it opened

"Whoa! What y'all got going on?" Jinx put his hands in the air. "Ebony, put that gun down. Aye B, what did you do?"

"Jeremy, please take me home. His bitch ass cut my face!" she shouted.

"That hoe got another nigga fucking her all in the ass and cumming in her mouth!" As soon as I said that shit I felt like a real sucker.

Jinx laughed. "Bounce, you sound like a sucker. Besides, you know she's way too jazzy for all that physical contact." He motioned her to give him the pistol and she did.

"Take me home!" she cried on his chest. He wiped the blood from underneath her left eye, then whispered something to her as he gave her his keys. She got her things and rushed out of the door.

"I should've known it was you!" I said to Jinx.

He pulled a blunt from his cargo pocket and lit it. "We had this conversation about Dominique?"

"That was after you quit messing with her. She was with Duck." I laughed. "That's what this is about?"

"I ain't tripping over Dominique. Shit, she fucking Buck. If an opportunity opens up for me to get even with him I'm taking it." He took a deep breath. "I bought your rims with Ebony's money. Plus, she ain't your main bitch."

"How long?" I asked quickly. I could feel myself getting mad. I felt like he played me and I honestly wanted to put hands on him.

He blew a thick cloud of smoke. "About three weeks ago, but it only happened once. Except for that night I put her down."

"That's crazy. So since she's a *Dinner Thief* she's fair game? Shit I guess I can fuck Staci or Mercedes."

He laughed out loud. "First of all, Staci wouldn't put herself out there like that and if Mercedes or even Ebony decides to fuck off, I know it's for my benefit. A hoe can't hurt me. I'm hurt when one of my guys reacts off of emotions, instead of realizing that Ebony Young is not Valencia or Catera-they're off limits. But a broad that you took from a dude she's been with for six years? A broad all of us had? You're mad 'bout that?" He laughed. "You thought she was wifey material?"

"And you don't?"

"Hell fuckin' no! I fuck with her because she chose me! I have a baby by my wifey. And I have a quarter piece in Knoxville that I love enough to give her the world. I have a couple joints that are crazy about me and they deserve bigger roles. But Ebony Young is only for entertainment."

He put the blunt in the ashtray. "You ready to fight about shawty? Hell, I should be the one trippin', you cut her face. That's my money you fuckin' with. All those magazines and video she has lined up. You could've played your role and supported her dream. You fools spend all that time around that nigga Buck and ain't learned shit!"

I laughed. "You're right."

"I know. Shit, shawty tryna put me in that new 'Lac truck, you damn right I'm puttin' this rod everywhere she wants it!"

He laughed as he tossed me a roll of cash. I stepped on the porch and watched him head to his car. I still felt salty, but I knew he was right. *Damn,I can't believe I let that bitch get to me. Fuck it, I'm too gangster for regrets. Plus, what goes around comes around*

Jinx

"THE LADIES' PICK"

"Brah's party is tomorrow night. I'm picking up my shoes right now." I turned onto Poplar Avenue, and headed towards Oak Court Mall. I was on the phone with Mercedes, but my mind was on shopping.

"Don't forget to bring my food and don't make me hurt none of these females when you get here," she said.

"Alright. Bye" I hung up and blasted my music. I zoned out and rhymed with my man Jay-Z about having *Girls*! *Girls! Girls*!

The mall was packed. I parked my Lexus near the back entrance and made my way inside. I had a little boutique I always shopped at. They sold only exclusives high-end designers and custom kicks. I was flirting with a couple of females when I spotted Angel pushing my daughter's stroller. Her mom and Amy noticed me first.

"Hey daddy's baby!" I picked up Angelica and she smiled. "That's my pretty girl."

"Where have you been?" Angel rolled her eyes at the trio of girls I was talking to.

I watched her mom and Amy going to the toy store.

"I had to handle something for Vago." I walked with Angelica as Angel pushed her stroller. "You look good in those jeans with your pink and white Jordan's on. I can't believe you have on tennis shoes in public. All those Giuseppe and Red Bottoms you make me buy."

"I bought these shoes like 20 minutes ago. Your spoiled ass baby refused to ride in her stroller, so I had to carry her." She wiped Angelica's mouth, then gave her a pacifier. "Gimme some money, since you've been with Vago."

"I left you $1500 this morning." She kissed my lips and smiled. "I saw something in Victoria's Secret that you'll love. It shows all my curves."

"Get that money from my cargo pocket."
"I love you." She tiptoed and kissed my mouth. "Should I wait up for you tonight?"

I put Angelica in her stroller.

"I'll be trapping all night, but I can take you to breakfast in the morning."

"I'll get Alexis to keep Angelica. I can dress up in that maid outfit and serve you eggs sunny side up."

I smiled. "Wear those pink stockings. I love you." I kissed her and our daughter. "Don't get broke."

"Boy please, I'm Jinx Vaughn's baby momma, if I get broke all I have to do is call him."

I watched as she pushed Angelica's stroller over to *Toys "R" Us*, then I went to get my shoes.

"Hello." My phone rang.

"Is this Jinx?"

"Yeah, who's this?"

"It's Victoria. Lucky told me to call you. I have some stuff you need to check out."

I turned and headed out of the mall. Victoria only boosted the hottest shit. If she called me, I had to go see what she was working with. I let her know I'd be there in an hour. First, I had to take Mercedes something to eat. I went to get pizza and wings for all the ladies at the beauty shop. I figured the shop would be crowded. It was a Thursday, but it was Memorial Day weekend. Plus, Hurk's party was 24 hours away.

"Damn boy, you look good with those glasses on." Cutie Pie wasted no time flirting with

me as soon as I stepped inside her shop.

I only smiled as she helped me put the food on the counter. Toya was sitting on top of the counter, August was in the shampoo chair, Vida and Ebony were under the dryer, and Mercedes was in Cutie Pie's chair. There were 15 or 20 more females and a handful of guys.

"Thank you handsome." Mercedes kissed my cheek after I'd given her a styrofoam wing tray.

August wrapped a towel around her head and then bumped me as she made her way to fix a plate. Toya peeped the whole thing, laughing and mumbling to Cutie Pie. Ebony saw it too, she rolled her eyes and whispered something to Vida.

"You ladies enjoy your lunch." I tried to leave as soon as I could but Toya had other plans.

"I hear you and your boys have a big surprise for tomorrow night," she said with a smile.

I knew she was trying to keep me from leaving trying to see if I could handle the pressure.

I smiled my usual cocky smirk.

"You never know what type of stunt we'll pull. You should stop by, let me buy you couple of bottles of Rose."

She put her hand on her hip. "Boy, you know I'm pregnant."

"Oh yeah? I just thought those jeans were lucky," I flirted.

"What'd you get Hurk?" Ebony asked after Toya thanked me for the compliment.

I noticed Mercedes rolling her eyes. "I got him tickets to see T.I and Lil Wayne in Nashville."

"Damn, that's love," Cutie Pie replied.

"How's Angelica?" August asked.

"Spoiled as hell. I just left her and her momma at the mall."

Mercedes decided to reclaim my attention. "Girl her lil honey colored eyes and curly haired self. They were twins the other day. I was kind of jealous."

"Staci should be jealous," Vida added sounding like the hater she was.

"N'all, Staci loves college. Besides, I wasn't trying to make Angelica," I said honestly.

"Anyway, I need to roll."

"Jinx, do you have one of those flyers for *The Bad Luck Girls*. My Uncle Bobo wants to put it on his website."

August had a smirk on her face and I knew why. She used a flyer as an excuse to walk me out to my car. We both knew damn well that Buck's little brother was doing a 37-month Fed bid for counterfeiting.

I noticed Toya wink at August as she led the way out to my car. "You got all your side hoes in there," August said once we were outside. She stood with her hands on her hips, her bow legs looked so good in the gold high waist shorts she wore. From the front, you could see her ass cheeks sitting phat.

"What I gotta do to get you out of those shorts?" I checked to make sure no one could see me, then I snatched her into my arms and kissed her until she moaned. "Come by my spot when you leave here. Bring a change of clothes too."

She stepped out of my arms and regained her composure. "I'd better get back inside."

I gave her the flyer and watched her walk away. "Damn, I'm good."

Chapter 4

Hurk

"THE PROTÉGÉ"

"Happy birthday shout out to my guy Big Hurk. My boy turned a dub today and the females came out to show their support."

Yellow Boy gave me a shout out as my guys and I entered the club. The place was packed, full of women with short skirts and dresses on and their toes were out. The ballers were there too, but all eyes were on me.

Toya bought me an exclusive Gucci set with matching loafers. I had on my *DTG* chain, a gift from my guys. My swag was through the roof, my glamour was up to par, and my smile was on beam. "The hoes came out tonight," I whispered to Bounce while I took a long look at the many dimes in attendance.

"Happy birthday big brother," Angel greeted me with a hug. She led me to the table where my gifts were. "1…2…3… Happy Birthday to you…" The entire club started to sing.

I laughed at the sight of my mom and Amy bringing me a cake from the back of the club. I lifted Amy up and let her kiss my face once the song was done.

"Help me blow the candles out," I said to her.

"Okay, cut her a piece so April can get her home." Buck pulled out a chair and told me to have a seat.

"I have a surprise for you my boy."

He clapped his hands three times and the spotlight was put directly on me. A trio of dancers came out of the center of the crowd and surrounded me. One was dressed as a nurse, one as an Indian, and the other one as a lady cop.

“Make it rain.” Lucky tossed a handful of bills in the air.

I just sat and enjoyed the show. I hadn't had a lap dance in a while.

After each girl gave me a private dance, Buck escorted me to his personal table. He poured us both a glass of champagne. “I'm proud of you. Real talk. Anyway, what do you have planned for the night?”

“Party and bullshit!” I replied.

“N’all you can do that anytime. I have another surprise.” He walked me to the VIP parking area. “You ever been in a Lambo?”

“Hell n’all! Where the keys?” I admired the black Diablo parked in front of me.

He tossed me the keys, but before I could open the door they both came up. Xaviera was in the passenger’s seat wearing a red bow around her breast and crotch.

“Happy Birthday, baby!”

“Go. She knows where. Enjoy your weekend.” Buck patted me on my back. Don't hurt him Xaviera.”

I got inside the car and tapped the gas.

“Shit, I gotta get one of these.” I looked over at my girl and smiled.

“Shit. I want some of that chocolate cake. I wanna fuck you while I drive this bitch. Make this is the best birthday ever!”

Chapter 5
Jinx
"THE PROTECTOR"

One week later

"Baby, your daughter wants you." Angel put Angelica on my chest.

I immediately covered my nose. "Damn Angel she stinks like a grown ass man!" I got up and grabbed a diaper. "You're too pretty to be so funky." She laughed at the faces I made while I changed her. "Damn, I can't wait til you're walking and talking."

"Don't forget we have to pick my stuff up for prom," Angel said when she came back into the room.

I finished changing Angelica, and then followed Angel into the den. "Stop sweating me about your prom, I got that under control. I bought your dress, my tuxedo, and the white on white Cadillac truck outside is your chariot." I kissed her lips. "I know how much this means to you, so imagine what it means to me."

"I hope Alicia wins prom queen. She's going with the guy you met at homecoming." She took Angelica from me. "I have to take Alexis to work. Are you going anywhere?"

"I have to take Slick a lil package. I want you to stay with me tonight." I took Angelica to the car and put her inside. Angel kissed my lips.

"I'll get Alicia to keep Angelica. I saw a new position I want to try." She bent over and grabbed her ankles. "See if you can hit my G spot like this."

I smacked her ass. "Don't forget whose car this is." I helped her into my new purple and tan CTS.

"Boy please, we both know this is my graduation gift. I love you."

I kissed both my girls, and then got into my Lexus once they were gone. I had to drop off a package to Cookie and Pasha for Hurk. He and Bounce were in Chicago with Buck.

Lil Mane was on the porch when I got there. He already knew why I was there so I didn't have to get out. He and I sat in the car and smoked a blunt, and then I was on to my next stop.

Lucky's sister, Vicky, had some new Louis Vuitton sets and I wanted to check them out. Plus, I owed her for the Versace dress I bought Angel to wear for her prom.

I pulled up and parked in front of her house on Rozelle. She was watching her dog use the bathroom. Victoria was an amazon with double D's, a ghetto booty, thick thighs but no fat anywhere. The way her white Gucci tennis dress fit her curves had me anxious to see what she had underneath. I'd slept with her twin, and both her mom and Aunt Debbie, but I always wanted Victoria!

"I saw those Maury sandals in Beverly Hills. I have a short set that will go perfectly with them." She looked me over and smiled. "You look cute."

I laughed while I played with her dog. "Gangsters aren't cute."

"That's your problem, you're too damn cute to be so damn gangster." She picked Muffin up and led the way into her house.

It was nice inside; everything looked expensive, all to the credit of her immaculate taste and tireless hustle.

I took my shoes off at the door-all her carpet was white so no shoes were allowed except in the kitchen and dining room.

"You hungry or thirsty?" She poured Muffin a bowl of water and herself a glass of grape juice.

"I'm good. I sat on the couch in the den and changed the TV from VH1 to CNN.

She rolled her eyes and sat on the couch with me. "I'm watching Love and Hip-Hop." She snatched the remote and changed the TV back.

"You're supposed to be showing me some clothes." I rolled a blunt while she headed towards her bedroom. When she returned, she rolled a clothes rack in front of her.

"Stop staring at my ass," she said.

"I can't help it."

"Anyway here, try this on."

I held up the yellow and pink polo shirt. "No ma'am."

She ignored me, handing me a pair of blue shorts with yellow and pink stitching. "I have a pair of blue and yellow boat shoes to go with this.

"I can't wear no pink," I said. When she didn't respond, I decided to at least see how this looked on me. I took my shirt and shorts off, then put on what she'd selected.

I couldn't help but notice the way she bit down on her bottom lip when she saw my half naked body. I took pride in my physique; I had a boxer's body.

"Yellow, pink, blue, and green are hot colors this season, trust me. I know what looks good on a man," she said.

I passed her the blunt. "That's why you don't have a man."

"Hmp... I don't need one, especially not one like your dog ass. As a matter of fact, my vibrator is larger and my toys make me cum harder."

"You fuckin' with the wrong cats then."

She mumbled something, then handed me a green and yellow polo set. "Hmp. I heard you messin' with Ebony Young and Mercedes. They'll have you broke or in jail cause all they're doing is sack chasing. Staci's not the ride or die type. I mean, she loves you, but she's not the type to settle for a dope boy or a gangster."

She laughed. "To be honest, Angel is the youngest but lil momma is the smartest girl you have."

"Let me find out you're scouting my squad. I can see you with a jewelry box on your hip."

She passed the blunt, and switched her way out of the room.

"You can't handle me Jeremy Vaughn," she said on her way out.

Before I could respond my phone vibrated. "Yeah, what's up?"

"Jeremy, Ziggy is over here drunk. He tried to kick the door in, now he won't leave."

"I'm on my way," I said and grabbed my keys.

I hung up just as Vicky was on her way back up front. I quickly changed clothes and let her know I'll be back after I handled Ziggy.

When I got to Staci's, Ziggy was sitting on the hood of his Magnum.

"Oh shit, it's Captain Save a Hoe," he laughed when I got out of my car.

"What's up with you brah?" He put his cigarette out on the hood of my Lexus, then tied his dreads behind his head.

"Fuck you mean what's up? I'm sick of you and that bitch. I came to collect on the debt. I

know she helped you rob me." Staci stormed out of the house throwing tennis balls and yelling at Ziggy. That fool slapped her so hard she spun around in a 360.

I beat him over the head with the butt of my pistol, causing blood to pour from his head.

"If you ever touch her again, I'll kill your soft ass." I kicked him in his stomach. "Get the fuck out of here and you better not press charges."

I checked Staci's bruises once Ziggy finally pulled off.

"It's cool baby. That fool won't touch you again. I promise you that."

Buck

"TEMPTATION"

I walked out onto the balcony of my penthouse in Chicago and took a sip of my Hen and Coke. My mind was on the million dollar deal I'd just completed. I felt good that I could still move and groove with the best of the best.

Chicago was a city that hustlers loved. It was a city rich in tradition and heritage, and known for the street legends it produced. I'd originally came to meet with my financial advisors, but I ended up running into an old acquaintance.

Cappie Loyd was an old-school boss. He earned his fortune in the 70's and 80's, spent all the 90's in federal prison, and after serving over 20 years he re-established himself as the most powerful man in Chicago.

He heard of me before we ever met. One of his guys was my cellmate in USP Big Sandy, I saved his life and in return he introduced me to Cappie. The two of us quickly grew close so close that he became a mentor and business partner.

My wife's phone call brought me back inside. She called to see how my meeting with him had gone. I let her know that I decided to buy the nightclub Cappie was offering, and that she and I would be spending the winter holidays in the Windy City. She let me know that Jinx had been arrested for shooting Ziggy Zaggs. I already knew, but like I told Bounce and Hurk, Jinx wasn't my concern. When I tried to take him under my wing he refused my guidance.

Maybe my hatred of him is what originally attracted me his ex-sweetheart. Either that, or the fact that Dominique was a dime. The why wasn't important, what was was the fact that she was also in Chicago.

I'd planned my trip around hers. I'd been seeing her since I met her at a basketball game a year earlier while she and Jinx were still dating. Out of respect for my marriage, we usually met out of state so Chicago was an ideal place.

"Damn you look amazing!" I stepped inside and let her enter the penthouse. "Pink is your color," I said while taking in every inch of her frame.

"Hurk and Bounce are here with you. Does Jeremy know about us too?" she asked.

I handed her a glass of champagne. "Doesn't matter? Unlike the cats his age, Jinx doesn't intimidate or impress me." I softly kissed her face. "I like you enough to care less whether anyone else knows."

"What about Toya?"

"She is exempt from that. Can you handle that respectfully?"

"I'm not sure. I'm used to being number one, my pride might get in the way."

She made her way towards the bedroom, kicking her pink heels off along the way. "Truthfully, if this is really what you want, then prove it."

I watched her unzip and step out of her dress. She got in the bed and spread her legs, allowing me the pleasure of seeing her pretty shaved pussy.

"I should be more than enough. All of this should be yours."

I kissed her lips. "It is mine."

"Come and get it then."

Chapter 6

Icky

"RELAPSE"

One month later

I sat on the trunk of my Crown Vic and watched the neighborhood. It was a hot June afternoon, plus it was Friday so the block was jumping. I'd just washed the car and was now waiting on Jinx to drop off a package.

In the time since he beat Ziggy, he'd been keeping a low profile. The only reason he was even coming by the house now was because he'd taken one of his side chicks shopping for her birthday. Honestly, I couldn't blame him for not showing his face so much since his name was ringing all over the city. Because of his rep for being violent his many girls, and the quality cocaine he sold, my lil brah was a hood star!

He pulled up at 3 o'clock driving Staci's white CLK. He got out and showed me love. "What's up Slick? Damn it's too live out here today."

"It's the hood. I thought you took your lil young joint to the mall? How you end up in baby's car?"

"She wanted to keep my car. Anyway, you talk to Hurk today?"

"He's with Tammy. Brah has that old pussy on lock." The two of us laughed.

We walked to the curb as a red Explorer pulled in front of the house. Foo-Foo got his fat ass out. "Serve me 1/2 ounce of weed," he said.

"This ain't no trap house nigga," I snapped.

Foo-Foo was Star's cousin, a young wildcat. He stayed in some shit, so I did my best to keep him away from my house. He started counting the ones, fives, and tens he pulled out of his pocket.

“My cousin told me you were here so I came over here.”

“Here.” Jinx reached into his sock and tossed Foo-Foo what he wanted to buy. “Let Lil Mane know I'm on my way.”

Foo-Foo got back in Explorer and pulled off.

“You know Vago caught a charge,” I said to Jinx.

“Who told you? Buck? It was only a brick soft and a lil .25, that's small.”

“I'mma rob him. Shit, I heard he got plenty work in that spot near The Fairgrounds.” I lit a cigarette. “For real, I put Gene and Wildcat up on it too. I'm just waiting for the right time.”

He looked at me like I lost my mind.

“Brah, that's crazy as fuck. Vago? And you talk about taking Gene and Wildcat?”

“Yep Bounce and Hurk going are to rob us afterwards, so I'm not worried about Gene or Wildcat.”

“Why brah?”

I looked him dead in the eyes. “Never get full. Ain't shit changed. The only reason you ain't with it is because you eat at their table. I'm trying to take the whole plate.”

While I was talking, a gold Acura pulled up. Mercedes got out and opened the trunk.

“Hey Icky. Here baby.”

She gave Jinx two Footlocker bags, and then kissed his lips. “I need some money.”

“You always need some money.” He reached into his pocket, and then gave her a small roll of cash. “Buy me something too.”

She got back in the car. “I'll call you later.”

“Aye, I like that outfit. That’s how I like to see you dressed, like a professional.”

“Thank you baby! I'm on my way to work. I’ll call you on my lunch break.” He watched her pull off, then handed me the bags. “That's 10 for you and big brah.” He showed me love before he got in the car.

“Slick, do you bro. If you want to knock Vago off, don't take Gene and Wildcat.”

"I hear you." I did hear him, but my mind was already made up.

Hurk

"BETRAYAL"

"Look at all this money brah!" Lucky said. "We rich brah, I'm 'bout to cop an Aston Martin, a money green joint!" Lucky popped a bottle of champagne. "Aye Bounce, you tryna to sell the Q45?"

Bounce finished stacking his money. "Nigga you better save some of this money. We'll have to play it smoothly til we see what Vago does."

"Fuck that nigga he locked up," Icky added as he put his money inside the duffel bag! I put mine up, and then dialed Xaviera's number. I hadn't talked to her all day. She and I had a fight the day before, and since she left my house I hadn't heard from her.

"She still ain't answering?" Bounce asked.

I was frustrated. "I'm going over there."

"Don't do it. Let her come to you," Bounce advised.

Lucky passed the Rose. "Let's go to the club," he suggested.

"I'm with that. Let's go to *JC's.*" Bounce stood and stretched.

"I'm going over Star's, "Icky said.

Lucky checked his watch. "I'm about to take Buck to the airport, but I'll be at *JC's* by midnight."

"Lucky, if Nyla calls let her know I'm with the Buck," Icky added.

We all headed out of Lucky's house and out to our rides. Real talk, when I first got in my car I was going home. But my heart led me to Xaviera's. Maybe it was the fact that I hated knowing she was mad, then again it could've been the fact her phone kept going straight to voicemail. Either way, I was knocking on her door less than 15 minutes after leaving my guys.

The TV was on, it looked like porn was playing. I could see through the crack in the blinds.

"Fuck this bitch doing?"

I could hear voices from inside. "Hold on Teresa." She opened the door dressed in only a belly shirt and a g-string.

"Oh my God, Hurk."

I forced my way inside. "What's up in here Xaviera"

"What up Hurk, you came to join the party," Playa Joe smiled as he stood naked, shaking a can of whipped cream. "Oh shit you didn't know."

"He does now," Xaviera said. "Anthony, I can explain."

I was in my car by the time she finished her sentence. I was fucked up! I loved Xaviera, despite the shit I'd done to her. I'd never expected she was that type of chick.

Fifteen minutes later, I was parked in front of *Bad Boy's*. His ice blue and gray Porsche truck sat in his usual spot, directly in front of the club.

"Welcome to *Bad Boy's* 380 Beale St., where everything is all good, especially if you're a bad boy, you dig." Youngblood was on the mic. I walked in and headed straight to Buck's table.

It surprised me to see August inside of *Bad Boy's*. She wore a sexy two-piece Gucci outfit and boots. Shawty was finer than the baddest video model!

"You pushing the Porsche truck?" I joined her.

She smiled. "My daddy took Toya to L.A. "You got your goon gear on-all black everything." She rolled her eyes. "You've been with Icky."

"I just left Xaviera's. I caught her with Playa Joe."

"He is fine." She smiled and asked me if I'd killed them. "She wasn't your type anyway."

"I ain't trippin'," I lied. "I am a Dinner Thief, I got too many females tryna get on the team." I threw up the *D.T.G* with my fingers.

"I see you OG Hurk. You lookin' trill up there with Ms. Davis. Never get full, ya dig." Youngblood gave us a shout out.

"Who started that?" August asked.

"Jinx and Icky. But, we got the name from this crackhead that Icky's mom knew. He told us that we hustled like dinner thieves and never got full. See, dinner is the most vital meal. You might skip breakfast and lunch, but fuck around and miss dinner and them hungry pains will make you snatch a plate."

She smiled. "I like that."

"We breathe this shit. I got that shit tattooed on my back."

She licked her pink lips. "I know."

"Hmp... I like where you have yours. Your daddy seen it yet?"

"Only Jinx and London have seen it. And you. And that girl that did it."

Youngblood gave Jinx a shout out as soon as he walked in. Lil brah had his T.I swag working; yellow and pink plaid polo shorts, a pink button up, yellow patent leather Jordan's, and a pair of glasses. August's entire demeanor changed.

"What's up gangster? Hi thickness." He showed me love, then kissed her nose.

"I was on my way to the house. Don't keep my boy out too late," I said to August. I gave Jinx dap, and then headed out to my car.

I'd had enough for one night, but tomorrow I'd make sure I made Xaviera hate herself for what she'd done to me. I was over one hundred thousand dollars richer. I could buy a bitch ten times as bad.

Chapter 7

Jinx

"LIL BIG BROTHER"

"Lucky's birthday is Wednesday. We're going out."

"Is it a couples' thing or just the guys?" Staci continued to clean my nails while I rested my head in her lap.

"It's couples' night. We're going to the Kanye West, John Legend, and Alicia Keys show." She kissed my face.

"I'm going shopping in the morning." She laid her night clothes out after I stood to stretch my legs.

I'd spent the past two hours letting her oil my scalp, clean my fingernails, and give me a facial.

"You sleep in that t-shirt every night. Why is it so special?"

She pushed me on the bed and then straddled my waist. "My granny gave me that shirt. I was 12 when she died." She put my hands on her hips. "I love you Jeremy."

"Trust me, I know that. I love your bad ass too."

A few tears rolled down her cheeks. "I'm pregnant. I found out about a month ago. I told my parents, now I'm telling you so you'll know. I wasn't going to say anything because I'm having an abortion."

"Get the fuck off me." I snatched her arm and pinned her back against the wall.

"Let me go Jeremy."

"Bitch, shut up and listen to me. If you kill my baby then they'll bury you too. I don't give a fuck if I have to move you back to Memphis and pay for your tuition myself-whatever it takes. You can't kill my seed Staci."

"But I can't."

I fought back my own tears from falling. "No buts. Trust me, we'll make it work. You won't have to miss school, I promise."

I walked her to the bed. "I love you Staci and I love our baby right now. Please baby? Please, okay." I gave her some kleenex. "Blow your snotty nose and smile."

"Shut up punk." She blew her nose.

"I love you so much."

"I love you more. Now, take a hot bath and lie down. I'll be back in a couple of hours to hold you and our daughter."

She smiled. "You want a girl; I want a boy."

"The men make the girls; we both know I made that baby." I kissed her again and hurried out to my car.

Like all Mondays I was making my rounds. I spent my morning with Angel and Angelica. We went to breakfast, and then took Angelica to the zoo to see the monkeys. My afternoon was spent at a photoshoot with Ebony. My evening belonged to Staci. We had dinner at her favorite Japanese spot, and then she made me lay up for over two hours. It was after 9 p.m. when I finally made it to Victoria's.

I was talking on the phone with August so I sat in the car for a few extra minutes. She was in Nashville. I was going up to see her the next night, so we were making sure our plans were solid. Once they were, I got out and headed into the house.

Victoria met me at the door wearing a pair of peach boy shorts and a white halter top. Her silky, black hair was in a long ponytail, the fresh jewelry box on her neck was on display!

"What's up booh?" She slipped her tongue into my mouth as we kissed.

She and I had been kicking it since the night I pistol whipped Ziggy. Ziggy didn't press charges on me that night, butVicky had my phone. She came and got me, and I spent the night and the entire next day digging into her guts. Since then, we've been creeping on the low.

I gripped her J-Lo booty and let her know how sexy she was. She led me to the couch and cuddled up under me. I listened to her tell me about her day. She'd gone to the gym and the spa, then she met her realtor about a building she wanted to lease.

"Maria and I are opening a boutique. She'll do hair and I'll sell my designs. We're calling it *Maria-Victoria*."

She fondled my nuts, then unzipped my cargo shorts so she could suck me off. I continued to play with her nipples while she did her thing.

My phone rang. "Yeah," I answered.

"Brah, we have an issue."

"Right now?"

"Yeah, Lucky merked a lil nigga in The Bay. Some Piru niggas tried to rob him," Icky said.

I bit my bottom lip as I exploded in Vicky's mouth. "I'll be there in 15 minutes." I hung up.

"Your brother killed somebody. I need to see what's up," I said.

"Okay, but first you need to put me to bed." She stripped and sat in my lap. "See, that dick ain't ready to go yet."

I guided myself into her hot pocket. "Act like you need it then."

An hour after taking the phone call, I was walking into Icky's den. My guys were dressed in all black, each one wearing mean mugs on their faces.

"Who was it?" I asked.

"Some lil niggas out of Ridgecrest," Lucky said. "I had been over Tierra's. When I got ready to leave, niggas tried to carjack me."

I turned and walked out to my car.

"Where you going?" Bounce asked.

"To The Crest. That boy Ant Hill run that mu'fucker. He knows what it is, he g'on answer for that shit. Niggas g'on start controlling their people, or they'll answer for um," I said honestly.

I got in my car and drove from South Memphis to North Memphis. When I got to The Bay I called my young chick and asked if she knew where Ant Hill was. She told me he was in front of the Ridgecrest Apartments. He never even saw me until it was too late. He was hugged up with some bitch.

I pulled up right in front of him and two of his boys, got out of my car and emptied all 17 shots from my glock into them. I wasn't trying to kill them, but if I did, oh well.

"Look at me bitch! No mask, no help. I'm in South Memphis every day, and I ain't hard to find. Next time you see a Dinner Thief, you either kill him or show him respect, but don't ever try a jack move because you ain't taking shit!"

I beat Ant Hill and his boys with the butt of the glock, and then I got in my car and pulled off as if nothing happened.

Chapter 8

Bounce

"JOYFUL PAINS"

One week later

"Uncle Bounce, my daddy took me and my momma to the zoo and my sister Bria went too."

Zion climbed on the couch and sat next to me. I was playing Madden in the den. I'd come by Zandria's to pick up Buck. Him and my sister were spending their usual weekly family day with my nephew. Despite all the time they spent together, I still had no clue how the two of them made Zion while Buck was in prison, nor had I asked.

"Let's roll, I have a meeting in 45 minutes." Buck came from Zandria's room and headed out the door after telling Zion he loved him.

"You drive," he said as he tossed me the keys to his car. Once we were in the car he dialed a number on his phone.

"I'm on my way. N'all, Bounce is dropping me off. Bye." He hung up. "Drop me off at Dominique's."

He lit a blunt, and then cracked the window. "Realize that the woman should be a perfect reflection of her man. If she's loyal, passionate, and God-fearing, you can teach and mold the rest of what you want. My wife was stripping at *JC's* when I first got with her, but look at her now."

"So you're molding Dominique?" I asked.

He smiled. "Something like that. I'm fucking her today though. Is that a problem?" he asked.

"It's not my business. That's between you and Jinx." I left it at that, knowing exactly how Jinx would react when he found out. Neither of us said much after that, we just smoked and listened to Yo Gotti's new mix tape.

When I parked in front of Dominique's townhouse, Buck got out and used his key to enter. I left there and headed to the studio. Icky was finishing his CD and wanted the original Dinner Thieves on the intro track.

It was so crowded at *Mic Check Studios* that I had to park in the vacant lot across the street. The music was loud and people were posted near cars. It looked like the club parking lot.

"What's up baby!" Lucky shouted as I crossed the busy intersection. He had the butterfly doors up on his Corvette. "Look at this. It's Yellow Boy's video."

I showed him love and then got inside the car so I could check out the footage showing on the dashboard screen.

Lucky pointed towards the stoplight. Jinx had completely blocked the flow of traffic. His tan and bronze Cadillac was sitting in the middle of the street. He burned rubber when he turned into the parking lot. His crazy ass parked next to us, then climbed through his sunroof. He had on a golden-brown Jordan shorts set, with gold suede Jordan's.

I laughed as he put his yellow diamond gold chain and watch on.

"You got this bitch on *First 48* tonight - killin' the damn scene!"

"Me? N'all, my shawty merkin'." He opened the door for Staci and helped her out of the passenger's seat.

"Damn," Lucky said.

"What I whispered?"

Staci wore a tight flesh tone catsuit with matching stiletto boots. She made Kim Kardashian look like Whoopi Goldberg.

She tossed her wavy blonde hair over her shoulder and showed all the haters the fresh jewelry box tattoo on her neck, as well as the yellow diamonds in her ears.

"Yeah, yeah I know," Jinx taunted me and Lucky. He knew he had the baddest chick out.

I spotted Valencia hugged up with Gooch Duncan. He was a few years older than us and a well-known hustler from Magnolia. He'd done a five-year Fed bid for cocaine conspiracy, but we all knew he was still doing his thing. Gooch was a real rich nigga, bought his first kilo of coke at 12 years old, had a Benz at 15, and went to the Feds at 18 for conspiracy to distribute cocaine. He'd been home over a year, but this was my first time seeing him, and here he was with my ex girl.

"What's up lil Kevion. I mean, Bounce." He greeted me with a smile and a firm handshake, signs of mutual respect.

"I see you haven't missed a step," I said, acknowledging his black on black Infiniti truck. "What's up Val," I spoke.

"Yeah, I hear you and your guys doing the most though," Gooch said.

"We a'ight. Just gettin' started. Anyway, let me go see what's up with Icky. Y'all be cool."

I hurried to catch up with Lucky and Jinx. "You cool?" they asked.

"Brah, I'm a mu'fuckin' Dinner Thief. I'll fuck around and hold that hoe hostage, see how much she's worth to him," I replied with an honest smile.

Buck

"GOOD GUY, BAD BOY"

"I'm not at home, but I'll be at the airport in the morning. How's my baby?"

"Craving fudge striped cookies and pickle juice. Anyway, don't make another one."

I watched Dominique as she walked back into her bedroom and got in the bed. "I love you, Toya. I'll see you in the morning."

Dominique straddled me and kissed my lips as soon as I hung up.

"Turn your phone off."

"I can't, she's pregnant." I sucked her naked breast. "Did you do what I asked?"

She smiled. "I saw a cute peach BMW. It was only $45,000."

"Only 45,000?"

"I am worth it, aren't I?"

I played with her hands and thought about her question. Was she worth the trouble I was getting myself into? True, she had the potential that Toya did at 19 or 20, but was she honestly worth everything I'd shared with my wife? I wasn't sure, but I wasn't quite ready to leave her alone either!

"You want the car?" I rolled her over and pinned her hands above her head.

She giggled as I nibbled on her ear. "I want you. I'm only settling for the car."

"I'll have Chong pick it up first thing tomorrow morning." I got up and got my clothes.

She got up and jumped on my back.

"I thought you were spending the night. I wanted you to sleep inside of me," she flirted.

"You know I can't stay all night." I flipped her onto the bed and smiled as she locked her legs around my waist.

She pulled me on top of her and kissed my mouth. She put her hands inside of my shorts and stroked me until I was hard. I snatched her boy shorts off and kissed her inner thighs. I'd never tasted her until now!

"Buck make me cum.

I brought her to two quick climaxes before I mounted her. She came again after three good strokes. Her pussy felt like it had bitten my dick it clamped so tight!

"I'm movin' you into a condo. Fuck yeah, you can get any BMW want." I stood up and held her in my arms, still balls deep inside of the best pussy I'd had ever.

She worked her hips and bounced herself on me, showing me she could hang with me.

"Oh shit, I can't stop cumin'." She bit my chest and screamed my name out loud!

"I'm not pulling out," I growled.

She kissed my mouth and moaned as I blasted her full of my seeds. I was still hard, so she rolled onto her stomach and raised her ass offering me her other hole.

"Yeah, you want to get me killed," I said with a smile.

It was after 2 a.m. when I woke up. She was snoring, a sexy smile on her face as she slept. I carefully slipped out of bed and took a quick shower before I got dressed.

"I'm gone. I left you some shopping money and I'll have Chung call you tomorrow about your car." I kissed her mouth and then headed downstairs.

When I get to the bottom of the stairs, I damn near shit my pants at what I saw, rather who I saw.

"What's up old-school," Jinx said. He was on the couch smoking weed with Xaviera and Yasmine, both of Dominique's roommates, in their bra and panties.

"It's all good," I replied.

He smiled. "I feel you, trust me, I know exactly how you feelin' right about now." He whispered something to the girls and they headed down the hallway. “Be careful out there,” he said to me.

“I can handle mine youngin'. I've been in the streets since you were shittin' green.”

He grabbed the pistol and box of condoms from the coffee table. “Yeah, these youngsters nowadays ain’t carin' though. Anyway, I gotta go give them two what I used to give that hoe upstairs.”

“Jinx, I'm not Ziggy Zaggs or Murder Mook.”

He sucked his teeth as he looked me up and down. “Yeah, you're a *Bad Boy,* Buck Davis, *The Good Guy*-Blackout Squad. The same cat that started the Committee of Thugs. The same cat that merked Alpo, Hollywood, and Pimp Fro.

He passed me the blunt.

“I respect your gangster, just respect mine.” He walked away without another word.

Hmp. Yeah, he's going to become a problem. I need to handle that ASAP, I said to myself, knowing that Jeremy Vaughn was not a wannabe he was a real gangster.

Chapter 9

Jinx

"BAD LUCK GIRLS"

Two months later

"I just got out of court, about to take Angel to get Miss Angelica."

I opened the door and helped Angel into the truck. I copped an Escalade a couple of months ago, but I'd upgraded it as a present to myself for my nineteenth birthday. It was white on white, with the chocolate interior, TVs in the head rest, dashboard, and visors. I spent thirty thousand on the wood grain paneling and alligator seats, and had it sitting on 26 inch Spreewell's- so when I stopped my rims kept spinning, ya dig!

I knew I was playing with fire. Hell, I was leaving court for a drug charge I caught on the fourth of July. I was in the hood with Lil Mane when I got caught with four and a half ounces of coke, eleven thousand in cash, and seven grams of hydro weed.

The case cost me over seven hundred thousand to get it taken care of. Zandria got me eighteen months' probation-a good lawyer is like oxygen, ya dig!

"You still coming over here?" Victoria asked. She was on the phone with me. I started my truck and pulled into traffic.

"Yeah, but I need to take care of something for Icky first."

"Okay I'll be back by then. Bye booh." Victoria hung up.

"You hungry?" I asked Angel before I handed her my phone.

She yawned as she let her seat all the way back. "I'm tired. Angelica had me up all night. Do you still want her this weekend?"

"I want both of y'all this weekend." I kissed her, slipping my tongue into her mouth when I did.

"That's how we got Angelica." She laughed as she rested her head on my shoulder. "I thought you were going to see Staci?"

"Her family reunion is in New York this weekend. Plus, I need to remind you where home is."

"And where's that?"

I smiled. "Where the heart is. You and Angelica will always be home. I got the both of y'all tattooed on my chest. Fuck you mean where's that?"

"Ooh boy. I love when you put me in my place. You just might get some this weekend."

My phone rang. "Answer that."

"Hello… Hi Mercedes. No sweetie, this is Angel, he's driving me to get our daughter." She covered the phone. "Baby, do you want the phone?"

"Angel, stop playing with me."

She kissed my lips. "Mercedes, he'll be over there in a couple of hours."

"Tell her I'll call her later," I said before Angel could tell me what Mercedes said. I snatched the phone and hung it up.

She laughed at how frustrated I was. "That's your hoe. Anyway, get out and go get my baby," she said, still laughing.

I parked the truck, got out, and hurried into the daycare center. My baby girl was sitting in the playpen, looking like a princess with her pink dress on.

"You happy to see your daddy. Your pretty self." I picked her up and kissed her fat cheeks. August walked over and gave me Angelica's diaper bag.

"She had a bottle like 30 minutes ago. How was court?"

"They gave me 18 months' probation. Anyway, what happened to you last night?"

She turned her nose up at me. "I called you back, but some girl named Meka Doll answered. Anyway, I'm sick of chasing you. It was fun while it lasted."

"It was," I replied.

After leaving the daycare center, I took Angel and Angelica to their townhouse in Covington. I moved them out of the city the day Angel graduated high school. Like I said, they were home, and it was my job to ensure their living conditions reflected that. I spent more time there than I did anywhere else. I stayed with them until they both fell asleep on the couch in Angelica's room.

My next stop was Icky's. He was on a promo tour with his group and had asked me to take Nyla some money for him. He'd moved to a plush four bedroom house in Southaven, Mississippi, far different from his trap house on Greenwood, in South Memphis.

"What's up playa," Nyla teased me when I got out. She and Koby were blowing bubbles on the front porch.

I handed her the Louis V. bag, then picked up my goddaughter.

"You are way too pretty to be Icky's baby."

Koby laughed as I tickled her belly. "Your booh just left," Nyla said.

I put Koby down. "Who's my booh?" I asked Nyla.

"Ebony. She had her back out, tattoo showing. I keep telling her that Staci can fight." She blew bubbles and smiled as Kobe popped and tried to catch them.

"I don't understand you. All of your boys fucked that girl; you, Lucky, and Bounce hit together."

I kissed Kobe, then hugged Nyla. I told her to tell Icky to call me, then I left before she started asking me about Icky and Star.

My next stop was Vicky's. I moved her out of the city limits to a little spot in Cordova. She pushed all her competition out of the picture. If Angel was the wife and Staci the girlfriend, then Victoria was the mistress.

I parked next to her gold Lexus coupe and got out. Other than her car and her red Tahoe, there were two other cars in the cove where she lived. I figured she had company, probably clients. Her and Maria were still a couple of weeks away from the grand opening of their salon boutique, but Victoria's clientele had grown.

"You're so damn handsome." She wrapped her arms around me and greeted me with a kiss when I entered the house.

I squeezed her fat booty. "Who is in there?"

"Yasmine, Val, Xaviera, and Vida. They came to get something for the Drake show. You lookin' so preppy. Getting your Carlton Banks on."

I led her by her hand as we walked into the den. I spoke to my home girls as I sat in the recliner. They all spoke back. Vicky played with my hands. She knew I had slept with each of them and felt the need to claim her territory. I was cool with it, in fact, I was glad she was making it known that she was mine.

"You heard from my girl Staci?" Vida asked, hating as usual.

"She's pregnant by me, I talk to shawty every day."

Vicky whispered in my ear, and then excused us as she led me to her bedroom. As soon as we were behind closed doors, I had her bent over, moaning as I kissed her panty-less ass.

"Hurry up and fuck me!" she said.

"What about your company?"

"They had their turn. You're all mine now booh."

Bounce

"GOOD AT WHAT I DO"

"Y'all, I need my shit like Hurk's was. The bad bitches came out for that fool." Big Lou passed me a roll of cash and the blunt he had been smoking. Mac Goo pointed towards Buck.

"I want what he's getting, ya hear me."

I smiled proudly, knowing my three mentors trusted me so much. I was in charge of promotions for three major events; Big Lou's 30th birthday party, Mac Goo's 15th anniversary party for *Small-Town Music*, and Buck's 35th birthday party.

"Bounce, you have seven more days, lil brah." Buck stood and led the way to the door. "I need to go check on my wife."

A cute petite chick got out of a champagne colored CLK. Buck hugged her.

"What's up Tammy Smith."

"My last name is Nelson punk." She punched his chest. "Hi Goo and Lou."

She hugged them too.

"Oh snap. Tammy, this is Zion's uncle, Bounce," Buck smiled after introducing her to me.

She looked me over and smiled. "You're Zandria's brother? Tell your sister to call me."

"You know my sister?"

Lou laughed. "You ever heard of Skip Nelson?" "Skip Nelson," I repeated. The name sounded familiar as hell.

Buck raised his shirt and pointed to the tattoo on his left side. "Skip

Nelson was part of the *Committee of Thugs.* He led the *River City Gunners.* That was my guy, Tammy's husband. You know Mace, from B.H.Z?"

"With the black and yellow Crown Vic? He went to school with Jinx's baby momma Staci."

"That's my son by Skip," Tammy said.

I laughed, realizing how small the city was. Mace bought work from Jinx on the regular.

"I need to talk to you," Tammy said Buck.

"It was nice to meet you," I said to Tammy.

She gave me a hug and a kiss on the cheek, reminding me to tell my sister to give her a call.

After leaving the *Tip-n-Skip,* I drove home. I parked my sky-blue Corvette in front of the house. I'd copped it a few weeks after we'd robbed Vago, the rest of my split was put for my unborn child. My cougar, Catera, was three months pregnant.

I went to my room and got my cashbox out the closet. I added the money from my pocket to what I already had.

"I need to call lil brah." I dialed Jinx's number and Angel answered.

"What's up B," she said.

I laughed. "Where lil brah?"

"With that stupid hoe. I mean with Mercedes."

"You cool with that?"

"I'm in his Lexus, with both of his phones and our baby is in the backseat, looking just like her daddy. The only thing Mercedes is doing is handling his business, maybe sucking his dick for a pair of Red Bottoms." She laughed. "Anyway, what you tryna to get?"

"Wow, you on the team now?"

"Boy please, that's why I let him have his lil bitches. I was just asking so I know what to tell him."

I laughed. "Let him know I need the usual."

"I sure will. Oh, I saw Gene today."

"For real? He dropped the charges after I agreed to pay for his hospital bills and rehab.

This nigga robbed me and I have to pay him because I tried to kill his dumb ass."

"Well, next time don't try. Anyway, I need to change Angelica.

"A'ight. Bye." I hung up.

Lucky walked into my bedroom dressed in all black. “Aye, I got a move. I need you.”

“What's up?”

He smiled. “You still in love with Val?”

“Val is *DTG*.”

“I know, but that nigga she fuckin' ain’t. Gooch got bricks and stacks on deck. Tierra saw that shit with her own eyes.”

I smiled. “Never get full then my guy. Let me suit up,” I said happily.

Chapter 10
Icky
"PAYBACK"

"I'm killin' everybody with an attitude. I'm just shell shocked." I joined Hurk on the trunk of his Crown Vic. "Too many people gettin' shot brah."

"I'm one of um." He laughed.

I watched Nyla's peach Charger turn the corner and pull into the driveway. After our big lick on Vago, I moved my family out of South Memphis. Two days after we moved, Star and I robbed a pawn shopfor $63,000 and some jewelry.

I moved to East Memphis for safety, so I wasn't too happy to see Nyla and our daughter at my trap house when she knew what was up.

"Don't start. Hell, I just left my mom's," she said as soon as she got out. "Go kiss your baby; I'm taking her over Cool's." I walked to the car and kissed Koby, careful not to wake her up.

"Now go and drop her off," I told Nyla.

"Why did you buy Star a house? And why are you taking her to New Orleans next month?"

I laughed. "You know why."

"Ugh! Don't get that bitch pregnant and you better be careful, that bitch talks too much.

All in *Cutie Pie's* braggin' about how y'all get money together."

I kissed her nose. "Long as that's all she sayin'. I'm tryna to put a baby in you though."

“Hmp, not ‘til I get the ring you've been promising for two years.”

“I'm trying to save up for it.”

“I can settle for something more affordable.” I pulled her into my arms.

“I love you too much to let you settle for less than the best.” She stepped away from me and got into her car. I knew she was upset, but I wasn't ready to settle down. At one point I was, but my life wasn't one that was appropriate for a wife and a kid, not yet anyway.

When Nyla pulled off, Sheena called. She was trying to get a nine piece. Since I didn't have it, I called Jinx. Twenty minutes later he pulled up in a red Altima. A sexy, short haired redbone climbed across the seat and pulled off no sooner then he get out.

He tossed me a backpack, then greeted both me and Hurk. Seconds later, August’s Range turned the corner.

“Aye slick, I'll come by in a couple of days and get the money. I'm taking August to

Tennessee with me for couple of days.”

“For what?” Hurk asked.

August got out and Jinx whispered something to her. He smacked her bubble butt and she got back inside the truck.

“I have to meet my Migo friend. Anyway, I'm out.” He showed us love, then left as quickly as he'd come.

I tried to convince Hurk to ride to The Mound with me, but he had to go check on his sisters. When I get to Sheena’s, the spot was crunk.

“Come out here and get this shit,” I said as soon as she answered her phone. I hung up and turned my music up louder.

Sheena was a hood rat, my little gutter bitch. She was tattooed and grilled up, looking like something out of an urban ink magazine.

“I got $5500, that's cool,” she said with a smile.

I couldn't help but laugh, she was full of shit.

“You still owe me from the last time. You’re trying to make me ask for some head.”

“It's worth it. Anyway, Nyla has your ass getting fat.”

She watched me do a little coke and she did some too. “I'm just eating well. You still fucking Pretty Toney?”

Her four diamond teeth sparkled when she smiled. “We just moved in together.”

"That's what's up." I read a text from Star. She was at her mom's. She and Gangster Greg just had a fight over some money he owed her.

"Aye Sheena, just give the money to Mercedes, let her know it's for lil brah"

"Okay, let her know it'll be tomorrow."

As soon as she got out, I smashed off. When I got to Stas mom's house, my girl was cursing on the porch with a bat in her hand.

"Bring your bitch ass out here!" she screamed.

I got out and Star gave me the bat. I noticed an ugly cut under her left cheek bone and I got mad!

"What happen?"

"That bitch hit me with an ashtray!"

"I was beating his ass." She wiped the blood from her face as Gangster Greg came out and headed towards us.

"You called his bitch ass? Yeah, I owe you for that shit you and your boys did at Ziggy's."

I moved Star to the side and tried to warn him. A few of the neighbors did the same-they knew I was not playing.

He swung at me, so I shot him in the stomach, leg, and ass!

"Stupid Ass."

Hurk

"NEW DAY, NEW WAY"

I parked my raspberry colored 645 in Cookie's driveway and got out. I'd moved her out of the hood and into a two bedroom townhouse in Olive Branch. I wanted to show her my new ride-flipping from the Jag to the BMW which was my reason for the late afternoon visit. She met me at the door.

"Ooh, let me keep it! C'mon, take me to the store." She snatched the keys and hurried out to the car. "What color is the interior?"

"It's olive green like your eyes." I pushed a button to let the moon roof retract.

"Damn, my juice box is wet. Pasha g'on love this car." She backed out of the driveway. "We have to go get her." She was excited to say the least. "When did you get this?"

I checked a text from Angel. She let me know Icky shot Gangster Greg. While I texted Lucky what Angel had just told me, I noticed the way Cookie was looking at me.

She took my phone and called her sidekick.

"Pasha, bitch guess what Hurk bought? A 645. You still at *Cutie Pie's*? We'll be there in fifteen minutes."

I smiled as I thought about how far I've come in eighteen months. I was only twenty- years-old, but I was worth over six figures, had two exclusive rides, Cookie and Pasha on my team, and a reputation in the streets that was solidified.

Just last night I hit a lick for $33,000 and ten pounds of kush. The week before that I got a cat for $28,000 and two assault rifles, and when I found out Gene and Wildcat robbed Bounce, I shot Wildcat six times. All it took was me getting shot and Strong Arm's guidance for the beast inside me to rise to the surface.

"What's on your mind?" Cookie asked.

"I want to take you and Pasha to New Orleans for Labor Day."

"Okay, I'll take the whole weekend off. I'll get Pasha to make the travel reservations." She turned into the parking lot of *Cutie Pie's* and parked next to Jinx's snow white caddy truck. Just as we were getting out, Jinx walked out of the shop. He showed us both love.

"I see you miss horse booty pushing this spaceship. You know Xaviera in there hatin'. Cookie headed inside while I sat on the hood with Jinx.

"What you got going on?" I asked him.

He told me that he wanted Angel to get her hair braided, so he brought her to the shop. He also let me know he'd spent the night with Dominique, Yasmine, and Xaviera.

"Why you telling me that?" I asked.

He smiled. "I'm too gangster to be a snake. I mean, I know how you felt about Xaviera but she's a Dinner Thief-and a cold freak!"

We shared a laugh. Cookie and Pasha came running out of the shop. I let Jinx know I'd call him later, then I got in the backseat so my girls could ride up front.

"Where we headed?" I asked.

"First, we're riding through South Memphis, and then we're going to the house so we can ride you," Cookie replied.

"Shit! Sounds like a plan to me."

I sat back and got comfortable, feeling like the gangster I knew I was. Ya dig!

Chapter 11

Buck

"INTUITION"

"The party was crazy! You heard about August and Vida?" Icky continued to laugh as he sipped his Remy. "She beat that hoe ass. That nigga Gutta Zed had to snatch her off Vida." I looked at him and then at Lucky. "What did you do?"

"We," Lucky paused momentarily. "Listen OG, it ain't our place to speak on it, but lil brah and August kind of messin' off. He took care of it, ya dig!"

Icky's car alarm went off. We all looked outside just in time to see Nyla knock his windshield out with a baseball bat. He rushed out to stop Nyla from doing any more damage.

"Nyla must know about him and Sheena Harris," Lucky said. He laughed as we watched Nyla chase Icky with the bat. "So, what's up with you and the MVP?" He relit the blunt Icky had put out.

"Dominique? Hmp, she's in excellent hands." He passed me the blunt. "I saw her BMW. What you g'on do about August and lil brah?"

"August is going through a phase. One day she'll want more than what Jinx has to offer. If not, then she'll find out the hard way that a father knows best."

He read a text, and then grabbed his keys. He had to pick Tia up from the airport.

The two of us headed out the house, I laughed at Icky and Nyla as I watched them kiss and make up. It reminded me of all the times Toya and

I had fought and made up. She'd never knocked my windows out; her method of payback was to spend crazy amounts of cash.

I hugged Nyla, then got in my car and left Icky's. It was shortly after 3pm on a hot August Saturday and I had a taste for a pecan pie.

"*Tip-n-Skip*, this is Tammy."

"Lil head, you got me a pie in the oven?"

"Mr. Davis, I do brownies on Saturday's and pecan pies on Sunday's."

"Act like it's Sunday. I'll be there in twenty minutes."

"You think I can pop one out of my kitty kat?" she asked.

"Ugh. That stale ass pie will probably come out dry and bitter."

She hung up laughing. When I got there, she'd already started making it. I walked into the kitchen and she immediately punched me in the stomach. I ran and she chased me out into the parking lot.

"You fuckin' Dominique. You were with her in the airport last night. At least she tried to disguise herself with a wig and some shades."

I stopped and thought to myself. "Who? How you know that?"

"My cousin works as a flight attendant; she sent me a picture on her phone. Please be careful, I don't want Toya to kill you or that girl."

"I have it under control. Anyway, let's smoke a joint til my pie is ready."

She rolled her eyes. "I can't get high with you. You know how I get. Anyway, I'll let you know when it's done. Call your wife or your booh."

"Damn I can't let Toya find out about Dominique," I whispered to myself once Tammy was gone. It was time to make a choice, but I had to be sure it was the right one or I could lose more than I could afford.

Lucky
"TAG TEAM CHAMPS"

"Where's your China Doll?" Kourtney asked.

"She went with Staci to get Buck's gift." She rolled her eyes.

"She's good at taking orders. Her good egg roll makin' ass." She finished changing our son.

"Keep playin'," I said. She laughed. "What you g'on do, hit me with another hammer? Break my other hand?" She picked Jr. up and bounced him on her knee. "I'm movin' to Boston with my daddy. I'll call you in a day or two so we can work out your visitation. I don't want or need your child support."

I was about to slap her smart mouth ass, but stopped when her Hulk Hogan looking dad knocked on the door. She gave him Jr., and then got the baby bag.

"I'll call you," she said.

Tia pulled into the driveway as Kourtney and her dad got in the car. She and Staci spoke to Kourtney.

"What's up?" Tia asked.

"Nothing I gotta take lil brah a package."

I kissed her lips, and then got in my car. I was mad as hell. I wanted to do something to Kourtney, but I wasn't stupid. She'd have me locked up. I've done ten days and she'd put a restraining order on me the last time I put my hands on her white ass.

My phone rang as I headed to my sister's. "Yeah," I said.

"Aye punk, my baby said don't forget to take care of Youngblood."

"I gave it to his other baby's momma, the finest one," Angel mumbled to herself. She hated Staci. "See, that's why Iysis is a dyke and Kourtney don't like you. I hope you break a toe." She laughed before she hung up.

Seconds later, I was parking my car under Victoria's carport. The peach Acura in front of the house looked familiar, but I wasn't sure just where I'd seen it. I peeped the AKA license plate and figured it was one of Vicky's sorority sisters.

"Aye Vicky." I entered the house through the side door, shocked to see London's sexy ass sitting at the kitchen table. "Damn girl. What your fine ass doing over here?"

She smiled and continued eating her grapes. I joined her at the table. "I came to get my outfit for the party," she said.

I asked about my sister to which she replied, "She's upstairs with your partner. I'm surprised you couldn't hear them, sounding like horny monkeys."

"Why you ain't up there? Don't act like you ain't wit it" I smiled for a couple of reasons- first; I knew London and Jinx were late night creepin', but also that she was fuckin' my sister too.

She got up and rinsed her bowl. "They were arguing at first. Besides, I'm a good girl."

I wasn't listening, I was too busy lusting over her and how sexy she looked in her white tennis skirt and heels.

When she walked into the living room her c-cups bounced like water balloons.

"Now you're a good girl." I put my hand on her hip and whispered into her ear. "You're stamped *Bad Luck Girl* and I know you love it." I softly kissed her neck.

She moaned as I lifted her skirt and touched her panty-less ass.

"Don't do me like this Lucky. You know I mess with Vicky and Jeremy."

I bent her over and pulled my wood out my Jordan shorts.

"That's how you doing my lil mama." Jinx stood in the doorway with a smile on his face.

"I couldn't help myself." I continued to give it to London. "Come help me keep her quiet," I said.

He walked over and kissed London's nose.

"You want me to help him? I wanna suck your dick," she moaned.

"Never get full," I grunted.

Chapter 12
Jinx
"THIS IS THE LIFE"

Two weeks later

"Boy, you're too cute, but you're still a baby." Cutie Pie flirted while she lined my mini fro and beard I'd been growing.

Toya joined in. "If I was twenty years younger I'd give Angel a run for her money."

"I'd wear both of y'all out right now, actin' like I'm not me," I said with a cocky smile. I didn't even open my eyes, but I could feel their eyes on me. "I love Cougars, I just don't go hunting because I'm too busy chasing paper."

Cutie Pie's phone rang. She turned the clippers off and went to get it. The other ladies and guys in the shop were talking amongst themselves, so I continued to flirt with Mrs. Buck Davis. She was sitting on top of the counter, facing me. Because she was wearing khaki shorts I could see every inch of her big yellow thighs. I can't lie, Toya was as sexy as any chick half her age and I've always lusted after her.

"Have, you talked to August lately?" I noticed her glance at the bulge in the crotch of my polo shorts. The sight of her thighs had me slightly aroused.

"You know her daddy told her to leave me alone." I laughed. "She came through the hood the other night though. Daddy can do a lot of things, but he can't scratch that itch, ya dig."

She stood up and adjusted the hem of her shorts- they'd risen into her crotch.

"You are really a mess. You know, if you hurt her you'll answer to me."

"I can't wait! Ain't nothing better than a well marinated rightly seasoned piece of red meat." I licked my lips and we both laughed.

Cutie walked over and gave me the phone. "It's that crazy ass Lucky."

"What up brah," I answered. He let me know that he needed a sweat suit, our code for a kilo. I let him know I would be in my spot in an hour. As soon as he hung up, I called Vago and let him know I was ready to bring him his money and re-up. I also let him know that instead of my normal twenty-five, I needed forty, to which he let me know he would be waiting on me.

"Here." I gave Cutie Pie her phone and a hundred dollars. "I'll see you in a couple of days so you can trim this shit down. Ms. Davis, it was a pleasure to see you again."

I made my way out of out to my Lexus. I wasted no time leaving *Cutie Pie's*, heading straight to get Vagos money. No one actually knew exactly how much work or money I was getting. For the past six months I'd been grinding, saving and stocking every dime in dollar. In nine months I saved $750,000, that's what I was about to spend with Vago!

"Ain't no looking back JV, no shorts, no losses, no fear... No mercy," I mumbled to myself while putting the money inside the duffel bag. "Let's get it," I said after zipping it.

Once I left Staci's I drove straight to Vago's spot. My nerves were on edge-riding with your life's savings would do that to you I guess. I didn't even turn the radio on, I just made sure I was following every law.

When I made it to Vago's, he and I-40 were on the porch. The two of them met me at my car.

"Follow them." Vago got into my car, while his brother got in the U-Haul.

"You come along way Jinx, proving yourself to be a very trustworthy and loyal fellow."

Vago admired the interior of my ride. "The life we live has been good to you."

I'm just trying to get it while it's good, shit don't last forever, ya dig."

He nodded with a smile, obviously understanding my point. "I can understand that. Which is why I wanted to personally let you know I may have to take a short vacation. But, I want our relationship to continue to progress."

I turned into a self-storage warehouse and followed I-40 to the back. He backed the U-Haul into the storage unit. Once parked, several guys appeared from both the truck and the storage unit.

Vago looked at me. "One of my spots was robbed a few weeks ago. One of my places in Miami was hit over a year ago. We initially suspected you, but after some thought and some close observation, we realize you'd never crossed us." He motioned for me to get out. The two of us made our way to the U-Haul. His guys were unloading it, but the drugs weren't what caught my attention. Vago's nephew and his nephew's girl were tied and gagged in the back of the truck.

"Only three people knew about those two spots, with the exception of me. One was an associate named Diego. The other was a guy named Boney and both were dead before I was deceived."

"So, your nephew did it," I played along, although I knew who'd done it.

He screwed a silencer on his gun. "Maybe... Maybe not... But he knew the ins and outs better than anyone. He showed her, she told someone else, so they must die." He gave me the gun, then motioned for his men to load my trunk with drugs.

Real talk, I was looking around, scared that the Feds were somewhere lurking. I'd seen too many gangster bios and read too many books; rats had no shame when it came to setting people up!

Vago sensed my hesitance. "I'm only looking at 36 months my friend. Besides, my own men would kill me if I betrayed our code. But I'm glad you're a thinker. It makes me feel better to know you understand the importance of every choice you make."

Spff! Spff! Spff! Spff! Spff! Spff!

I shot the nephew and the bitch before Vago could finish his sentence. He spoke to his guys in Spanish. They immediately went to work, cleaning the truck and disposing of the bodies.

Vago led me to my car. He asked me how much money I was riding with. I told him. He told me I only owed him for the 25 this time, but from now on I pay for 40.

"There's about to be a drought. You should prepare for it."

"No doubt," I replied. "I'll be in touch," I said as I shook his hand. "Make sure he get to his destination without any issues," he said to one of his guys.

"Go," he said to me.

I got in my car shaking like a smoker in a crack house! Once again, I killed for them and once again they made me rich!

Hurk

"ONLY THE STRONG"

I sat on the floor of my bedroom, shaking like a pair of bad dice. I just got in from a crazy night.

"2 bricks, 10 pounds. Bitch ass nigga," I mumbled to myself, proud that I robbed Pretty Toney. I caught him leaving the strip club, and laid his punk ass down.

My phone vibrated, bringing me out of my zone. "Hello," I answered. "Big brother, my booh should be pulling up any minute now."

I headed to the front door. "What he coming here for?"

"Because it is raining and he left his glasses on the dining room table. Anyway, my baby is stinky, bye." Just as Angel hung up Jinx was running up to the porch.

"What up gangster," he greeted me.

"Fuck you been?" I asked.

"Had to take August to the house. Plus, I need to take Terio a lil package." He dialed a number on his phone.

"Where you at? A'ight."

He put the phone back inside his pocket. "I'll be right back."

I watched him rush out to a white car. Seconds later, he came back inside.

"Ooh… Mercedes gettin' fine!" He put a bag on the floor and then sat on the couch. He put several kilos on the table. "That hoe can't do shit for me except hold or run some work. Strictly on payroll," he said honestly.

"I hear you pimpin'."

He laughed. "Your sister's the one pimpin' All she has to do is take care of Angelica, go to school, and keep them suckers out of her face. I got her for the rest of her life. I'ma marry her when she graduates."

"Are you serious? What about Staci?"

He put five bricks in one bag, then five in another. "Staci has a boyfriend. The nigga been buying a lil work from me and was braggin' about his lil chick from Memphis. I asked him to let me see a picture, it was her."

"Staci? Hell n'all!" I laughed.

"She left Ziggy for me. I ain't trippin', that's why I got Victoria and August."

I laughed so hard I had tears rolling down my face. "And you talking about wifin' Angel."

He slid me half a brick. "I hear you been hanging with Slick."

I took my pocketknife out and cut that bitch open to for a taste test. "Can't nobody hang with Slick. Damn, this shit is pure."

"You hear that?" he asked. We both reached for our guns and crept to the door.

Bocka! Bocka! Bocka! Bocka! Bocka!

Chapter 13
Jinx
"GOOD DADDY"

Three days later

"Have you heard from Hurk since he left the hospital?" Vicky massaged my shoulders while she sat in the small of my back.

"He's at Pasha's. You excited about tomorrow?"

She stood up with a glow in her eyes. Tomorrow was the grand opening of *Maria-Victoria*.

"I'm too anxious. You'd better come by there too."

I kissed her lips, then get up and stretched. "I'll be there. You g'on be here tonight?"

"I'm going out with my twin and our sorority sisters. Male strippers!" She pulled a roll of cash from her bra.

I pulled her into arms. "I want you to come over my house when you leave. We can have a slumber party"

"Okay, I'll call you."

I put on my shirt and shoes, and then gave her a few hundred before I left. I rode through South Memphis. It was the first of the month which meant collection time!

"Aye lil mane, I'm out here G."

"Here I come."

I sat in my Lexus and texted Angel while I waited. She wanted me to stop by one of her friend's house when I finished handling my business. Lil Mane came out and gave me the money he owed me. I gave him a couple extra ounces of coke. He was my guy, I loved to see him shining. In my opinion, he'd be the guy to take the *Dinner Thief Gangsters* to the next level. I had to help him earn his name, ya dig!

When I left there I went to meet August. She was at the nail shop and called for some money. I took her a couple hundred, and then left. Ebony was there and she and I weren't on good terms. She'd been dating the star point guard for the University of Memphis.

"Hi baby, I was just about to call you."

"I'm outside."

Angel laughed when I turned the music up. "Come get your big head baby and turn that music down."

I hung up and headed inside the house full of women and kids. I was as polite as possible, but I was in and out in a couple of seconds. "You seem frustrated. Which one of your hoes pissed you off?" Angel went through my phone the way she always did.

"I fucked off $6700 this morning."

"That ain't shit to you, but how'd you lose it?"

"Dice game. I should've just put it in Angelica's account like I started to."

She looked at me like I'd lost my mind. "What account?"

I pointed to my glove box. "As much as you rumble through my shit, I can't believe you didn't find this. I put money in there every week." I gave her two bank statements.

I smiled as I looked back at my sleeping baby. "I put up money for you too. I never know what might happen." She was quiet for a couple of minutes.

"What are we Jeremy?"

"You know what it is. The whole town knows." I held her hand and smiled. "You're my angel."

"Look at her." She turned and put Angelica's pacifier back in her mouth. "I can't wait til she's walking and talking."

I looked at them both and smiled. "I can't wait til you have her little brother or sister."
"Boy stop." The two of us laughed as I continued to drive home.

My evening was reserved for Angel and Angelica. When we got to the house, I fed Angelica before the three of us took a bubble bath together. I then laid in the bed with Angelica, while Angel took her mom some money.

When she returned, Angelica was asleep, and I was weighing bags of weed while the money machine counted the day's profits.

"Baby, have you seen Bounce's motorcycle?" She sat in my lap. "You g'on buy me one?"

"You buy it."

She kissed my mouth. "I want you to buy it for me. Ooh, and I saw a pearl white M3 I want. We can trade in my car."

"You just got a damn truck." I pinned her on her back and bit her neck. "You think your lil pussy is that good."

"I know it is. And it's all yours. Anyways, I texted Victoria and told her you'll see her tomorrow."

"That's crazy."

She unbuttoned my shirt. "Yep she'll be a'ight because tonight, this dick is all mines. I'ma take you to heaven booh."

"Say no more then. Shit, we can practice making Lil Jeremy."

She pushed me on my back and pulled my shorts to my knees. "No baby. I'm swallowing all the kids tonight."

"You g'on get a car and that damn motorcycle." I laughed.

Chapter 14
Icky
"THE TRAP"

One month later

I had been in the studio most of the day working on the last couple of tracks for my mix tape. I looked at my watch. Realizing it was later than I thought, I shut down and made my way downstairs and out to my car.

"You Ike Turner," a white guy in a suit approached me as soon as I stepped outside. His demeanor screamed detective.

"Who's askin'" I replied.

His black partner got out of the Buick Regal. "I'm Detective Moore, this is Detective Wilson, we're from robbery and homicide and would like a few moments of your time."

"Call my lawyer." I unlocked my car door.

The white cop laughed. "Aren't you Slick Icky?"

"That's my rap name."

"Look, you jackass, I know you're responsible for a lot of bullshit. You're a real chip off the old block... like father, like son," the black cop snapped.

I stepped in his face, but held my composure. "I don't play about my pops."

"We know, that's why you killed your Uncle Boney. Who called that shot, your dad or Buck Davis?"

I spit at his feet. "Fuck you want, my nigga?"

"Some information. Does the name Sherwin Akins ring a bell? You probably knew him as a Soldier Blacc. You met him through Sheena Harris, he was your old robbery partner until he disappeared."

"It was unsolved, but had your coward ass connected to it!" the white cop added.

I lit a cigarette. "Y'all need some pussy. I'll see y'all in traffic."

I got inside my car and turned the music up. N.W.A. rhymed my thoughts, *Fuck the police*!

"You'll slip Icky, it's in your genes to be a jailbird. The Mexicans know you crossed them."

I pulled off immediately. The comment about the damn Mexicans terrified me so much that I drove straight to Buck's.

When I got to Buck's house, he was home with Toya and the kids. He cursed me out for not calling first. When I told him about what happened he advised me to lay low until he found out what was up.

I was about to pull off when August pulled up in Jinx's truck. "I hope you ain't had no niggas in brah's truck."

"Ugh, I hate your stupid ass. You hater."

"You ain't shit but a lil sack chaser. You betta hope Jinx don't find out you fucked Hurk."

She smiled. "I'll make my daddy hate you."

"Hoe, I'm Killer D's son. You need to fuck harder or suck slower because the only reason

Jinx mess with you is to make your daddy mad."

I got in my car and smashed off. If August wasn't Buck's daughter I would've kidnapped and raped her dumb ass. My phone started ringing when I pulled off.

"Hello," I answered.

"Brah, I told Lucky and Hurk to meet us at *JC's*. Two detectives asked me about the Mexicans. We might need to lay low for a minute." Bounce repeated what Buck said. He let me know he'd tell me more at the club.

We needed a plan, something solid because if the cops knew about us robbing Vago, there's no telling what Vago knew-or worse, what he had planned!

Jinx

"GANG BANG-BANG"

I stood on my porch and watched the traffic flow. A couple of my workers were handling the hand to hand sales, several others were on security, while Lil Mane and I kicked it on the porch.

I'd turned my little street into a one-stop shop. You could get whatever you could afford; coke, weed, pills, or pussy!

"Jinx, why you don't serve crack?" Lil Mane asked.

"I can't cook it," I laughed. "Plus, I hate the hassle. I'll come out better doing what I do plus I gotta let niggas eat some kind of way." I laughed as the lil homie and I shook hands.

I watched as a gold colored Range crept towards the house. My phone rang, it was Toya calling to scc which house was mine. I stepped off the porch so she could see me.

"Get in," she said with a sexy smile.

"What's up? What you doing in the hood after dark?" I said.

"Boy please, I'm from the hood. Anyway, I came to get something to smoke."

"You smoke? Damn, let me find out Mrs. Buck Davis has a little hoodrat in her."

She ran her nails across my face. "There's a lot about Miss Toya Davis you'd be surprised to know. Anyway, I need the same thing you gave August yesterday."

"You don't want that." I gave shorty nine inches and a hard time.

"She rolled her eyes. The girls your age actually like the way you come at them?"

"I'm honest to a fault, either you hate it or you love it. I just see no reason to beat around the bush and I can back up whatever I say." I pulled the half ounce of weed from my stock.

"Here, you don't owe me shit."

I got out.

"You look good tonight, that baby filled your face out more."

"Bye Jeremy.

I stood on the curb and watched her pull off. Not even thirty seconds later, Lucky's Corvette pulled up. He got out and showed me love. I was concerned being about him in Castalia. The hood was saying that Lucky and Bounce robbed Gooch for a couple of kilos.

"Fuck that nigga," he replied. "Anyway, I came to tell you what happened to the fool Pretty Toney. You know him and Terio got to fighting at *JC's* last night."

While Lucky was talking I noticed a dark colored SUV speeding down the block. Seconds later, gunfire erupted from every direction! My lil soldiers quickly responded, but before the truck turned off of Lapoloma, Lucky was hit in the foot and Lil Mane was hit in the shoulder.

"Val, get them to the Med, ASAP!" I yelled. "Don't worry brah, on the gang, I'll handle this shit personally."

Chapter 15

Jinx

"GROWN MAN SHIT"

One month later

It was an unusually warm November afternoon. It was sixty-seven degrees in the city, so I decided to take Angelica to the park. My baby girl loved the ducks at the pond, and with her walking and talking a little, I loved seeing her chase and quack at the ducks. With all the hustling I've been doing, I needed some time to chill and relax. And what better way than a day with my daughter.

"Quack-quack daddy!" Angelica laughed and pointed at the ducks. She kissed my cheek, and then resumed her quacking.

While I was watching Angelica I got a call from Lucky. It had been a month since he and Lil Mane got shot. We still didn't know for sure who did it, but we suspected it was Gooch who sent those guys. Lucky wanted me to let it slide, but Lil Mane wanted revenge and I was with him.

"I'm at the duck pond with my baby girl."

"Duck pond?" He laughed. "I figured you were too gangster for that."

"You know Angelica is my soft spot. Anyway, what's up?"

"Shit, just left the studio with Icky and Bounce. You talk to big brah?"

I laughed and proceeded to tell Lucky about Hurk and August. She told me that she'd slept with him a few months ago. I was in shock, I mean, a few months back he'd walked in on her naked at my house so I knew it was bound to happen. I was more salty because he still hadn't told me. Maybe because he shot-off after three or four strokes.

"Hoes ain't shit!" Lucky said.

I gave Angelica a box of apple juice, then watched her refocus on the ducks. "She's only a woman," I said to Lucky referring to his comment about August. "That's why she's a side bitch. Plus, Buck was pushing for her and Hurk to hook up."

"But look, I'll be at the club tonight, you coming through?"

"N'all I'm chillin' tonight. I'll call you though," I said. "Don't forget we have that meeting tomorrow. Love lil brah." We hung up.

I let Angelica play for a few more minutes, then we left the park. She'd fallen asleep as soon as we got inside the truck. So instead of taking her to the mall, I decided to surprise my mom and drop Angelica off there.

Although Major Vaughn and I still weren't on speaking terms, Angel and my mom insisted that my daughter have a relationship with her grandparents. I loved my mom too much to deny her that. Plus, it wasn't her I had an issue with.

"Ooh she looks just like you today! Look at Granny's angel face." My mom grabbed Angelica from the car seat.

"You wanna keep her tonight?" I asked after kissing her cheek.

"Of course I do. I can take her to church with me. I just talked to your sister. She and Elliot are coming to dinner on Thursday."

"I'll be at Staci's, then Angel's mom is cooking too. But if you make me a pecan pie I'll stop by here." I smiled, hoping she wouldn't pressure me too much about the family dinner. I still wasn't ready to deal with Major Vaughn.

She kissed my cheek. "I'll agree, if you promise to let Angelica spend the day with me Thanksgiving."

"I can do that, just let Angel know." I gave my mom Angelica's diaper bag, kissed them both, and then headed home.

I was a block away from my house when I get a surprising phone call.

It was Toya!

"You busy?" she asked.

"On my way home. Why, what's up?"

She was quiet for a moment, and then she blew my mind when she said, "Listen, my husband is in Chicago and I'm horny. Are you ready to back up some of that cocky shit you been talking?"

"Ain't but one way to find out." I pulled into my driveway and said, "I'm at the house."

“I'm on my way.” She hung up without another word.

Bounce

"DINNERTIME"

"Aye Sonya, c'mere." Yellow Boy continued to call for Sonya, but she ignored him.

She made her way to me, kissing my lips to let everyone know what it was.

Sonya was the lead singer in an R&B group called "Kiss," but she was also crazy about me. I met her at the studio one night I was with Icky. She was recording a song with him, and as soon as I saw her, I had to have her. That was over two months ago; two months of wild, crazy, kinky sex!

"Let's get out of here," she whispered.

"I'm waiting on Jinx. But as soon as he gets here I'll be ready to go." She whispered. "If I were you, I'd call and cancel. I'm going over Beauty's. She wants you to come with us." She winked her eye at me, then walked over and joined her best friend.

As soon as she walked away I dialed Jinx's number.

He answered on the second ring. "Something came up G, I'll have to do that favor tomorrow."

"I have something to do too. I'll just call you in the morning."

I hung up and made my way over to Sonya and Beauty.

"You all ready?" I asked.

They followed me out of the studio and out to my car. The three of us got into my Infiniti and pulled off the lot.

"And Bounce, I hope you can handle both of us I can be a little demanding," Beauty said from the backseat. She was exactly what her name suggested a true natural beauty.

I couldn't wait any longer. I pulled the car into an empty lot and parked. I not only let my seat all the way back, but I did the same to Sonia's seat.

Beauty climbed over the seat and removed her jeans and shirt.

"You like?" she asked, in reference to her naked body.

"Damn right I like." I leaned back so she could sit on my face, while her sidekick pulled my rod from my jeans.

A smile spread across my face. I couldn't help but feel like the gangster I was. I knew how that boy Future felt now. Two bad bitches at the same damn time!

Chapter 16
Jinx
"WOMAN SCORNED"

Thanksgiving Day

"So, Jeremy I hear that you may be moving to New York. I take it the modeling business is doing well." Staci's dad smiled as he passed the cornbread muffins to me.

"I'm not moving, but I am leasing a condo in Manhattan and business is doing great."

Staci handed me a glass of water and put a couple slices of turkey on my plate.

"Two of his models were featured in the latest Vibe magazine. Him and his partner will be on TV next week."

"That's wonderful. So, I guess child support won't be an issue for you," Mr. Armstrong said to me. I was insulted by his comment, but I was used to it. He never really liked me since I told him Staci was having my baby. He'd been extra rude.

"I'm the one that moved Staci to Harbor Town and I'm the one providing for her and the baby. I love your daughter and our baby."

"I'm not saying you don't or that you haven't made the proper preparation, but let's not pretend your lifestyle is the safest."

I could only smile. I've sold him grams of coke, now he had the nerve to insult me like his shit didn't stink! I wiped my hands and my mouth.

"With all due respect, I've taken care of Staci for the last 18 months. I pay her car note, her rent is paid up for three years. I pay her tuition and whatever else she thinks she wants."

I looked at both of Staci's parents. "You don't have to like me, but I've earned your respect." I kissed Staci's nose, then thanked her mom for a wonderful dinner.

"Jeremy. Wait! I'm coming with you." Staci pulled my arm as I headed out to my truck.

I looked into those gray eyes and smiled.

"Your family is coming. But, I tell you what, I want you to spend the night with me and Angelica."

"I thought your mom had her." She rested her head on my chest. "What about August?"

I laughed. "That's nothing. And my mom wants me to come by her house, so I'm going to pick up Angelica while I'm there."

"I love you Jeremy, fuck what my dad said."

I kissed her lips. "I'm your daddy. Now, go feed my seed."

When I left Staci's I went to Hurk's moms. Angel, Alicia, and their mom prepared a huge meal.

Lucky and Icky were in the front yard smoking weed when I parked and get out.

I sat on the truck because I was on the phone with Victoria. She was in Miami with Sugar Momma, her aunt, and sister. Trey Songz and Usher were having a concert and Vicky won front row seats. I'd been sitting in the driveway for ten minutes before I finally got off the phone and off of the truck. I greeted my guys like I normally did with our D.T.G handshake.

"Your baby mama is shinin' on everybody in the house. Bro, you drove little Angel crazy," Lucky said while passing me the weed.

Hurk joined us. "Go get her lil brah." He took the weed from me, and then pushed me towards the door.

I could hear Angela as soon as I stepped into the house! Alexis hugged me, and then led me into the kitchen. To my surprise, my daughter was in her highchair, face covered in cranberry sauce and dressing.

"Hey mama." I picked her up and kissed her face. "You got your tan Nike suit on, with your little messy face." I walked over to Angel. "You went and got her? I told you I would."

"You must didn't get my message. Your mom brought her over here because Major Vaughn was at home. You need to tell your side bitch to let you answer your phone!" Angel snapped.

I laughed. "You need to calm down. Better call and talk to your boyfriend like that."

Alicia finished setting the table. "Jinx your pie is in the oven and the one your mom left you is right here."

"'Preciate you little sis." I finished wiping Angelica's face, then I gave Alicia $100 for my pie.

"Give me my damn baby!" Angel snapped at me.

"Say what?" I asked Alicia to hold Angelica, and then I escorted Angel out onto the patio for a private conversation. "What the fuck is your problem?" I asked.

She folded her arms across her chest and rolled her eyes at me. "I'm cramping and I'm sick and tired of stupid ass, lying ass lil boys."

"So. You know I don't care about you and your boyfriend. You chose that nigga."

I smiled as Angelica duck walked her way out to us. "It's cool," I told Alicia when she tried to stop her.

"You act like your taste in women is impeccable, all them scalawags and trifling hoes," Angel added.

"Okay and? Who had my first born? You have my heart, you know everything, got keys to everything, access to everything. You and everyone else know damn well you and Angelica are number one in my life."

"I want to be the only one. I'm more than enough."

I pulled her over to the swing and held both her and our daughter. "Concentrate on school and on our daughter. The rest of what you want or need will fall into place." She sucked her teeth, then took Angelica inside. I sat alone for a few minutes, until Icky joined me.

"I'm having the same issue with Nyla."

"Ain't no situation, I love the fuck out of Angel. She still young though, still growing.

Hell, I am too."

"N'all, Vicky got your ass sprung. She got you dressing like a New Yorker weaing Timbs and Coogi, fitted caps and shit."

I brushed off my cinnamon colored Timbs. "Angel is my heart. I mean, I love Staci too and Vicky, but Angel is so far ahead of them."

I laughed. "What's up with Nyla though?"

“I hit last night, but she wouldn't let me spend the night.” He pulled his powder pack out and did some.

“She's tired of your cokehead ass. You, Bounce, Hurk, and Lucky got too much going on and that habit is not a good look.”

He got defensive. “You're the only one with dope charges.”

“Because I'm too friendly. Y’all catching bodies and attempts, I'm chasing a million.”

“Who pistol whipped Ziggy? Who shot Super Dave and Mo-B?” He did more coke. “I feel you though, niggas need to be smoother. Buck said the same thing.”

“Fuck all that. For the gang’s sake, we need to keep gettin' money. That Buck shit is on y’all. Anyway, I got a pie to eat.”

He showed me love before I headed back inside. I loved Icky, but something in my gut told me he was headed down a dark path and I wasn't sure I could travel it with him.

Lucky
"BINGO BANGO"

I sat at the table and watched the VIP lounge. I was in *The Honeycomb* for a special Thanksgiving ladies' night and it was fire marshal packed! The vibe was sexy, as were the women, and I was the only Dinner Thief in the club.

"Is that Lucky?" Vida asked. She was with Nyla who spoke as she sat in the booth with me.

"I can't believe you're alone," Nyla said.

I tapped my hip. "I'm never alone. Anyway, does Slick know you're in here with this tiny ass dress on?" I asked after I noticed how tight and short her dress was.

She smiled, knowing she was fine as hell. "Ike Turner is not my man. I'm sexy and single." She high fived Vida.

I poured us a glass of champagne. "So you and your sidekick are on the prowl?" I asked.

"Boy please, I'm a dime and a diva." Vida mugged my face and smiled. "Speaking of sidekicks, where's Miss Tia?"

"Does it matter?" I asked.

"Damn, excuse me!" she replied.

Nyla laughed. "I can't believe you and Tia Pham. Out of all the females chasing your pale ass," she added.

"Shawty has most of these hoes beat head over heels." I spotted Ziggy Zaggs from across the club. "Tell that fool he needs to walk lightly," I told Vida as she stood to leave.

"Long as he's with me he's safe," she said as she left me and Nyla alone.

Nyla let her hair down and finished her glass of champagne. "Roll some kush," she said while refilling her glass.

"Ain't no smoking in here," I replied. I couldn't help but notice her body language. I wasn't used to Nyla looking or acting sexy. She and I had been friends since pre-school; our moms were best friends. Now here she was with her titties sitting up, thighs showing, looking like she was ready to serve that vagina on a platter.
"Do you allow smoking in your house?" She rubbed my face with her long nails,

grooving to Maxwell's *Sumthin' Sumthin'*.

I had to put an end to her flirting. "Aye Nyla, I love Slick. I can't take you to my house to

smoke no weed."

"Why not? We've been friends since we were three years old. I'm the same girl with the pink lips that cut your ponytail in the second grade." The two of us laughed at the memory.

"You're lucky I had a crush on you. Sugar Momma and Aunt Debbie beat my ass for that."

"Ooh, poor baby." She pinched my cheek. "C'mon, I want you to get me high... Besides, I rode here with Vida and she's not ready to leave."

I reluctantly got up and followed her out to the parking lot. I hit the ignition on my keypad and started my S550. "Who you texting?" I asked.

"I let Vida know I'm with you." She grabbed the blunt from the ashtray. I snatched it before she could light it.

"That's not for you," I said.

She sniffed it, then cursed as she tossed it out the window. The blunt was Icky's and it was laced with coke.

"Your robbing ass, junkie ass partner must've been in here. Hmp, he turned you out too?" she asked in reference to the laced blunt.

She lit the blunt I handed her.

"First of all, that wasn't mine. Secondly, brah was your booh a few months ago, ain't no need in talking shit now." I pulled into traffic and cracked the window.

"Anyway, Icky is a custo, a cold cokehead. All he does is rob and get high. Him, Bounce, Star, and Val. Oh, you know Star's pregnant."

I didn't comment on any of that. Instead, I chose to change the subject. "I thought Slick had a deal with Def Jam?"

She texted on her phone. "He missed the meeting. Hmp, he left Koby with that bitch

Tierra yesterday."

"For real? I need to talk to brah."

The rest of the ride was silent except for the radio and Nyla texting. When we got to my place it was drizzling outside.

"Make yourself at home," I said. She kicked her heels off and walked around my living room.

"You have a nice place. You live alone?"

"Yeah, but Tia helped decorate the place and my kids are here every weekend."

"I took this picture." She pointed to the photo of me and my guys from our trip to South

Beach. "I was pregnant and evil." She laughed. "Wanna know a secret?"

I sat at the table and rolled a blunt. "I'm listenin." "I wanted to fuck something so bad... I let GG Tate lick my pussy in the stairwell."

I'd just lit the blunt and choked when she said that shit! "Jinx said that too! Hell n'all! You are too wild."

She removed her leather coat. "Lucky, I want you. I know you love Icky, but I don't. And I hope you'll give us a chance." She stood over me. She was so close that her breast touched my head. "I want to be Lucky's lady."

I tried to think about anything other than Nyla slowly undressing in front of me, but it was useless once she dropped that purple dress and stood totally naked.

"You got a baby by my nigga."

She dropped to her knees and pulled my dick out. "It's Thanksgiving. Let's make this a night to be thankful for."

"Fuck! Ahh shit! Just tonight." I grabbed her hair and leaned back on the couch.

I was playing with fire and if or when Icky found out, he'd either burn me or Nyla. But that's something I'd deal with later, right now I was gonna deal with shawty and be thankful for the opportunity!

Chapter 17
Bounce
"GUESSING GAME"

Two weeks later

"Lucky got the boot off today. He's on the way up here." Icky sat in the barber chair and took his fitted cap off. "That fool got a new bitch he been creepin' with. He stood me up yesterday. I ended up with Trevor and Youngblood."

I noticed the way Jinx cut his eyes at me. He obviously knew exactly who Lucky was fucking with. All of us knew but Icky. I found out a couple days earlier when I caught Nyla leaving Lucky's spot in Whitehaven. Hurk saw Nyla in Lucky's Impala a day later, and Jinx found out from Staci.

"Tia probably had him watching Lifetime," Jinx commented. He was texting Angel while Maria twisted his hair.

"Y'all stop hatin' on my lil brother," Maria added. "Anyway, Bounce I hear you and Smurf are getting closer. I thought Catera was the only one?"

"You could be number one." I pinched her booty and laughed when she hit me in my chest.

Hurk walked in with his sisters Alexis and Amy. "What's up gangstas." He greeted each of us before he sat down in one of the empty seats.

"Where you comin' from?" Icky asked.

"I took them to the mall. We still on for tonight, right?"

Jinx stood and stretched. "I'll meet y'all at the club. I need to check a few traps." He paid Maria and headed to his car.

Hurk let Maria know he'd be back in a couple of hours. He had a meeting with Buck. I walked with them out to the parking lot.

"I thought you were waiting on Lucky?" I asked Icky. He pulled his powder pack out and did a little. Jinx shook his head, then got in his car without another word.

My phone buzzed. "Hello."

"May I speak to Kevion?"

"What's up Smurf?"

"You busy?" she asked.

I let her know I was leaving *Maria-Victoria*, headed where she was. She was in South Memphis at her nephew's pee-wee football game, and asked me to pick her up. It took me 45 minutes to drive from the boutique salon to South Memphis. Smurf and I were going to the race track. It had been months since I'd seen my home girl with her modeling and me with work.

I picked up Smurf and drove out to Millington. We used the drive to catch up. I told her that my son was due in February; she let me know she was ready to start her own family.

"You know I've missed this, kickin' it with you."

I smiled at her comment. "I missed you too."

"Remember the homecoming dance 11th grade?"

"I remember we fucked in the bathroom. I think I remember you rented a suite at the Marriott. You wore that sexy ass two-piece dress. That was the first time I ate pussy."

She smiled proudly. "Aren't I special."

"You still is and you always will be."

I parked by the racetrack. "You know, I still regret the way we broke up."

"Me too I always hoped we'd get back together and have our happy ending," she said.

I held her hand. "We can always make today the first day. I mean, I have a baby on the way, and I kick it with Sonya, but you know how I feel about your lil tiny ass."

"Okay I'd like that. Now, let's go watch these races, you know speed turns me on."

Icky
"STREET POISON"

"Lucky and I just left *Melanie's.* I took the lil bitch your package too. How'd you get back in court though?"

"Crack law. Anyway, tell your momma to send me some pictures. I love you lil nigga."

"I love you too, Killer D. Tell my brother I love him."

"A'ight Bye." My dad hung up.

I took a deep breath and slowly exhaled. I was stressing over some messed up news I'd received. There was a rumor that my dad was about to testify on Vago and a cat named G-Baby. The news not only shocked me, it was embarrassing. I had this niggas blood in my veins!

"You straight brah?" Lucky passed me the Rose bottle and let his seat back.

"I'm stressing. Nyla's bitch ass fuckin' with some nigga out The Haven. The hoe brand-new."

He laughed. "Brah, you got Star. Fuck Nyla brah."

I hit the powder and then started my car. "That hoe got $80,000 of my money at her house."

"Shawty is a Crump, she don't need your money. I'll talk to her, she'll give it to me for you."

I did the last gram of my coke. "Jinx got work?"

"I can call him." He flipped his phone out. "Angel, where lil brah? Ask him can I call Shawty." He laughed. "Tell him it's for a friend of mine ok, bye." He hung up. "Call August or Mercedes."

I dialed August's number. "Hello," she answered.

"Aye, brah told me to call you. I need something personal."

“He told me not to deal with you.”

“What? Hoe, quit playin' with me!” I snapped.

“Hoe? Your powder head ass. Your lil dick ass, that's why your baby momma fuckin' GG Tate. Sissy ass... And your daddy is the police, bitch.” She hung up on me.

Lucky looked over at me. “What happen?”

“That bitch said she ain't dealin' with me. Something bout lil brah said not to.”

My phone rang, I answered on the third ring. “What's up with you brah? You called August?” Jinx sounded irritated about me calling his bitch. I'd let him know what I called for and August snapped.

“I told his bitch ass exactly what you said!” she replied. “Shut up,” he told her. “Slick, I told Shawty not to fuck with none of y'all like that. If you and brah ‘nem g'on get high, I can't sponsor that,” he added.

“Dig that then Big Tymer.”

“See, that's that shit I'm talkin' about. You bout to act a damn fool instead of respecting what I said.”

I lit a cigarette. “Nigga respect these nuts! You got this bitch relaying messages and shit. She fuckin' Hurk. Her sack chasin' ass.”

“Slick, this is me brah. Chill out with all that loud talkin'.” “Fuck you, pussy ass nigga. Matter of fact, I'm on my way over there. I'ma beat your ass today.” I hung up.

“What happen?” Lucky asked.

I made a u-turn and headed to Castalia. I was on my way to Jinx's. “I'ma beat that bitch,” I said.

“Y'all trippin',” Lucky laughed.

Ten minutes later I was getting out of my Crown Vic. Jinx was sitting on the porch. His nonchalant attitude made me even more upset than I already was. As soon as I was in striking distance I punched him in the face.

Lucky grabbed me. “Fuck is wrong with you Slick?”

“Watch out Lucky.” Jinx tossed his shirt on the ground, then gave Lil Mane his pistol.

As soon as Lucky stepped aside I rushed Jinx. He hit me with so many punches that I fell backwards into the street.

“Get your soft ass up, actin' like you really want to fight. You know what's up with me. I'ma break your face out here!"

I got up and swung a wild punch, he countered with another multiple punch combo to my face.

"Jeremy... Stop..." Angel grabbed him and I got in a good punch that cut him underneath his eye.

Whop! Whop! Whop! I was dropped by three punches I never even saw. I was laid out in the middle of the street high and bloody as fuck!

"Go get your gun sucker." He looked down at me, and walked away.

Chapter 18
Hurk
"GET MONEY"

One week later

I sat at the table in the far corner of *Tip-n-Sip* and waited on my guys to show up. I called an emergency meeting to iron out our issues. It had been a week since Jinx beat the hell out of Icky, but since then Lucky and Bounce had fallen out too. According to Jinx, Bounce paid Sugar Momma for sex and when Lucky found out he went postal!

Jinx was the first one at the diner. He walked in with a smile on his face and August on his arm. He greeted me and asked August to cut him a slice of pecan pie. She spoke to me and then made her way toward the kitchen.

I sipped my orange juice and waited until August was gone before I said anything. "What's up with you and her?"

"I took her to the fair this morning." He smiled when she returned with his pie.

"I'll call you when I get off work." She kissed the corner of his mouth before she left.

I couldn't help but laugh at the look he gave her when she was gone. I started to let him know I'd slept with August, but he cut me off.

"I already know, it's cool, brah." He laughed. "She said you couldn't hang. How you think Lucky talking ass found out?"

Bounce walked in and joined us. "Where the other two?"

"Brah, what's up with you? You used to be paper smooth, now you're tougher than He-Man?" Jinx continued to eat his pie, even as he said, "That cocaine got you chemically off-balance."

"Who you s'posed to be?" Bounce snapped at Jinx. Jinx just smiled, but I knew he was strapped so I intervened.

Bounce got up and walked out of the diner, Icky had just pulled up. Bounce said something to him before he was able to get out, then got inside his car and pulled off, with Icky right behind him.

Jinx read a text, and then let me know Lucky wasn't coming because he was with Nyla.

"What do you have up for the night?" I asked Jinx.

"I'm with you," he replied.

The two of us headed out to my Navigator and got in. I flipped the truck from teal and blue to brown and beige. I also added three more TVs – from 2 to 5, and my sound system was over $10,000.

"This bitch is going to murder the car show." Jinx admired the Louis Vuitton interior and oak wood paneling. "Yeah, Pasha and Cookie got you on point. He read another text. "Aye, take me up to *Cutie Pie's* so I can drop this money off to Angel."

I pulled into traffic just as Buck and his wife were turning into the lot. "Did you handle that?" he asked, referring to Lucky and Bounce's drama.

"Not yet," I replied. He mumbled something, then pulled into the lot.

I pulled off. "You should talk to him about Slick," I said to Jinx. He continued to count his cash. "That ain't his business." "Whatever. Anyway, I need a brick. What are you going to charge me?"

"You need to let me give you about five of them. I keep on telling you I'm on for real."

I laughed. "I just need one. I got 18,000."

"18,000? Brah, I'm gettin' $32,000 easily... But, for you, I'll work with that. Just give it to Angel."

He checked his phone. "I'm outside now," he answered."C'mon."

He hung up. Thirty seconds later, my niece and sister walked out of *Cutie Pie's*.

Jinx got out and picked his daughter up. "You look pregnant," I said to Angel.

She rolled her eyes at me. "This sweater is supposed to fit like this you fat head bastard," she added.

"Quit cursing in front of her." Jinx put the cash in Angel's hand, kissed her lips, then passed Angelica to her. "You wanna go to the movies tonight?"

"We can. I'll get Alicia to keep Angelica. Oh, I told Lil Mane to leave that money in your mailbox. I'm not going to South Memphis with my baby, not in your car. One of your hoes might shoot at me." "I love you," he said as he got in the truck with me.

We left the shop and rode through South Memphis. I had to collect the rent from the guy living in my mom's old house. An old-school Crip named Criminal lived there now.

"The whole fucking hood over here," I said to Jinx when I parked the truck. The two of us greeted the familiar faces as we made our way into the crowded house. He must've been having a party. It was in the fifties but the loud music and the smell of charcoal was strong.

"West up lil niggas. Aye Jinx, take that slob ass shirt off." Criminal laughed in a drunken slur. He was in the *Hoover Gang* and he hated red!

Jinx removed his red St. Louis Cardinals sweatshirt.

"Yeah, we partyin', gangbangin', and terrorizin' lil yellow niggas like you." Criminal played with Jinx's hair. "Shit! long hair don't care! You got your little dreads and shit."

Jinx slapped Crim's hand away. "Chill out!" he said firmly.

I spotted Murder Mook in the corner of the room. To avoid any trouble, I suggested that we go outside to talk.

"Aye lil nigga your momma a'ight?" Crim asked after giving me the rent money. I let him know she was cool. "Yeah... I see you hanging with your brother-in-law the nigga puttin' dick on lil Angel. That pussy got good to him," he sipped his gin and laughed.

Jinx slapped the bottle out of his hand. "Watch your mu'fuckin' mouth!" he snapped.

I stepped between them.

"Let's go," I said to Jinx.

Reluctantly, he got in the truck. "I'm killin' that fool," he whispered no sooner than I pulled off. "The only reason he still breathing right now is because you were with me."

"Nothing seen, nothing said," I replied.

He looked at me with the cold stare. "N'all, that fool will be an example. Ain't nobody disrespecting Angel.”

Buck

"BACKSTABBERS"

"I'm telling you Buck. Them lil niggas you got runnin' behind you are not straight. Keep um out of your wax" Gooch whispered.

The two of us and Nacho were inside *Tip-n–Skip*. They came by to tell me what the streets were saying concerning the *Dinner Thieves*, and it wasn't sounding too good. Nacho leaned over the table and whispered, "The lil Fatima bitch told me Lucky sold my chain to some dude in Detroit. My lil folks said he saw the young nigga on YouTube with my shit on, but it was deleted when I checked it."

"I'll see what's up." I paused as I watched Tammy walk into the diner.

"Bad boy, I'm ready," she said matter of factly, her tone let me know she wasn't feeling my meeting with Nacho and Gooch.

I let the fellas know I'd look into their inquiries, then I led Tammy out to my car. She was busy putting on her makeup by the time I got inside my 645.

"I called and told Toya you were taking me to the airport. She said she'll be at the house by the time you get there."

"Okay. Listen, when you get to Chicago make sure you get in touch with Cappie," I said.

She pulled her sweater over her head and started to change clothes. I noticed a small tattoo of a baby on the back of her shoulder.

"It says peanut," she said as if she could read my mind. She took off her heels and jeans and put on a more comfortable sweat suit and Jordan's.

"You still think about that?" I asked.

She braided her hair into a ponytail. "I was 13 you were 15. It hurts so bad that my little cootie pop swole up for three days. But, you let me ride your face, so I was cool."

"You tasted like water." I laughed. "You got pregnant your first time, did you tell anyone?"

"Toya. That's my best friend, I tell her everything. I even told her about Miss Dominique."

"Who Toya? What the fuck?" I asked.

She rolled her eyes. "Boy please, that young ass girl is not worth all the trouble you're getting yourself into. You bought that bitch a BMW." I turned into the airport entrance. "I love you, but don't hurt my friend. She was there for you every day of your bid. Don't throw that away." She kissed my cheek, then got out of the car. Strong Arm carried her bags and they headed inside.

I stopped and got a few pizzas on my way home. To my surprise, Toya had yet to make it home. I was just kicking off my shoes when I got a call from Gooch telling me that my daughter had a fight.

"Yeah OG, she beat up that lil broad Vida, and that boy Gutta Zed poured motor oil all over her and her car."

I grabbed my pistol as I ran out to my car. It took 15 minutes for me to make it to *Mic Check Studio*. There was a large crowd in the lot. August's red Acura with cover in oil and she was too, though she'd managed to protect her hair and her face.

"Where is he?" I asked as soon as I got out of my car.

"He left with Playa Joe. They went to Orange Mound."

Jinx pulled up and called for August.

"Go home and get yourself cleaned up," I said to my daughter. I gave her my keys.

"I got this," I told Jinx.

"Oh yeah?" He laughed.

"Call me if you need me," he said to August before he pulled off.

I threw August's car in reverse, then sped out of the lot and into traffic. The tires were slick, but I was like a NASCAR driver behind the wheel. On my way to The Mound I called my boys Hoover Duke and Front and let them know what was up. Just as I anticipated, Front was already in Orange Mound. I spotted Gutta Zeds black charger in Melrose Park.

Bocka! Bocka! Bocka! Bocka! Bocka!

I didn't say a word, I just jumped out blasting until he fell. At first, a couple of cats acted like they were ready to help him, until they saw Front and Duke aiming assault rifles at the crowd.

"You g'on kill me in front of all these people?" Gutta Zed laughed.

I hit him with my gun until he cried.

"Help! Buck Davis trying to kill me! Buck Davis is trying to kill me!" he yelled. Suddenly, shots were fired at me. Me and my guys shot back as we scrambled to our rides.

"Shit!" I noticed I'd been hit in my left hip. I smashed on the gas and the car swerved. The light changed from green to red. As soon as I hit the brakes I remembered the oil on the tires. The car fishtailed and crashed into a utility pole.

"Oh my god! Are you alright?"

"Get him out, his car is on fire!"

I faded out, smelling the smoke, and feeling my gunshot wound as well as the injuries from the crash.

Part Three

Chapter 1

Lucky

"NOT LIKE THIS"

Three months later

I slowly got out of bed and made my way to the bathroom. I was in pain, a direct result of all the bullshit my body had been through. In the past six months I had been shot, stabbed, and pistol whipped. It hasn't been a week since I was robbed leaving the club. It was only $22,000 in cash and jewelry but they beat the shit out of me! I stood in the mirror and took a look at the ugly scar under my left eye.

"Damn they tried to fuck me off. Hatin' ass niggas."

After a hot bath, I got dressed to leave. Today was Nyla's birthday and the two of us were spending the afternoon together. We've been kicking it on the low for the last few months, but since Icky knew about it we'd started to be more open. Quickly, she'd become my favorite girl!

Tia and I still did our thing, but she was too far gone for me. And both my baby mama's were on some new shit. Courtney took Lucky Jr. to Boston and Iysis took Latrell to Atlanta.

Before leaving the house, I went into the backyard to feed my dogs. My two pitbulls jumped and barked as I poured their food into their bowls. I rubbed their heads, then carefully stepped out of their cage. I dusted off my green suede Jordan's, then headed to the garage. I got inside my clover green Chevy on 26's – the car matched my Japanese denim shorts and tan t-shirt.

As I pulled out of my garage I called Nyla to let her know I was on my way. She was at her mom's in Bunker Hill. I had to take the long way to avoid Castalia because I shot Nacho a few weeks ago when we were in Atlanta for All-Star weekend.

Ms. Crump's spot was jumping. Their home had been the spot for as long as I could remember. All the Crumps lived within five minutes of each other, and there were plenty of them!

"Ugh. You ain't Nelly. Got that big ass bandage on your face," Nadia, Nyla's sister, checked me no sooner than I stepped out of the car.

I hugged her and then complimented her hairdo. "I went out with your brother the other night. It was cool, but his baby momma kept texting him" she said. "She has a tracker on his dick. It was good but I can't handle that baby momma drama."

"I know how Angel is," I replied.

Nyla came out the house wearing a sexy two-piece skirt set with green heels. I pulled her into my arms and kissed her pretty pink lips.

"My momma wants to talk to you," she said. She led me up the porch.

"You got my baby pregnant," Ms. Crump pinched my arm soon as I was in reach.

I laughed as she chased me around the front yard. "Chill out woman. If she is pregnant, you know I got her." I handed her three hundred dollars to go get a bottle and celebrate

"I'ma a kick your ass Renzo Mendes. Your mannish ass is just like your damn daddy. You look like him too," she said.

I looked at her like she'd lost her rabbit ass mind. "My daddy? You know my daddy?"

"Do I? Boy, Bad Boy is your daddy. He ain't tell you?"

My stomach dropped to the bottom of my feet. "Who told you?" "I used to live with Sugar Momma and Pimp 'Fro. That's how me and your momma met him. Bad Boy was crazy about your momma until she met her husband."

I was really fucked up about it, but I played it off. "Oh, yeah, that's right." I checked my watch. "What's up, you ready?" I asked Nyla.

"Ma, I'll pick Koby up in the morning." She got in the car and reached for my hand. "I'm so sorry for that."

I forced a smile. "You're cool. I just need to talk to my momma and

Buck." I reached underneath my seat and grabbed her birthday gift. "Happy birthday!"

She opened the Macy's bag and pulled out the two Gucci clutch purses. "Ooh. Spoil me baby." She kissed my lips. "Thank you Renzo."

"You're welcome. Anyway, are you pregnant?"

"I'm a few days late. I have an appointment for Monday morning. You wanna come?"

I smiled. "Do you want me to?"

"It depends. What are we Lucky?"

"I'm not sure. What do you consider us?"

She turned the music down and turned towards me. "I consider you my man. I mean, you

pay all my bills, you take care of Koby, and you make my kitty kat purr." She laughed at her own silliness. "I love you, Koby loves you."

"I love y'all too," I said.

Nyla and I spent the day enjoying each other's company. It started with lunch on the patio at her favorite deli shop. Next, we went to see one of those chick flicks she loved. I went down on her while the movie was on, then I gave her some birthday sex when it was over.

It was after 7 p.m. when I finally left her place. She was going out with her girls and I had to talk to Victoria about what Ms. Crump told me. I pulled up at Vicky's and parked behind Jinx's chocolate and white Escalade. He won the truck from a cat in Houston at a dice game. Him and my sister opened a nail shop in Houston and were getting a lot closer.

"Put some clothes on." I covered my eyes when my sister answered the door in only a pair of white boy shorts.

She walked upstairs and I joined Jinx in the den. He passed me the blunt he was smoking. "You been with Nyla?" He laughed. "Slick said he saw your car at her house."

"I heard some crazy shit today," I said. I paused. My sister put on a T-shirt and was now sitting in Jinx's lap. "I heard Buck is my daddy."

"I know you're glad you didn't fuck August," Jinx joked.

"Who told you that?" Vicky asked. She was dialing a number on her phone. "Sugar Momma, you need to get over here. N'all, Lucky wants to ask you about his daddy. Okay." She hung up. "You want a drink, something strong because you need it."

"So it's true?" I asked her

"I'll let Sugar Momma tell you."
"Well make my drink a double," I said.

Hurk
"SPRING FEVER"

"You heard from lil brah?"

Angel continued to fry her chicken while answering, me. "He should be here in a minute." She chewed a small piece of the chicken and then fed it to Angelica who was sitting in her highchair eating mac and cheese.

"Why didn't you tell me Bad Boy was Lucky's daddy?" she asked me.

"Say what?" I asked.

"Yeah, Nyla's momma told him, but I was on the phone when Sugar Momma told him the truth." She fed Angelica some more chicken. "Sugar Momma lied to Buck when he first asked. She told him Lucky was a trick's baby because the man had money. Then when Buck got locked up, she lied because she thought he would never get out."

"That's your problem, you talk too much." Jinx kissed his baby girl, then smacked Angel's ass.

"What's up gangster," he greeted me.

"I need some 4-bars," I told him. "What she talking about?"

"I'll let Lucky tell you. Anyway, I got the bars. You need something else?" he asked with a slick ass smile.

Angel rolled her eyes at him as he fixed Angelica's dress. "No, he does not," she snapped.

"Chill out. Matter of fact, go change her diaper." He handed her the baby. "Ask Lexis to keep her for me."

"Where you going?"

He kissed her mouth. "I'm taking you to Houston with me. I gotta go see Vago, ya dig. His uncle wants to meet your nosey ass."

"Me? Why me?"

"Because you're my shawty. He invited us to his birthday party. G'on now, our flight leaves at 11:45 tonight."

I laughed as I watched my sister walk to the back. "You two are perfect for each other. You about to meet the plug?"

"I been met him. He wants to meet Angel. I keep tellin' you, and them people love me! I can give you 10 bricks right now; you won't owe me a dime." He checked to see if Angel was around. "I got a little bitch in The Bay, Tameka. She fuck with Tino Dillard. I got her gettin' off 10 brick a month."

I laughed, but declined his offer. I let him know I had some counterfeit money – I got from Buck.

"I want it," he said. "I'll give you $20,000 and 500 Xanax. I got 4 1/2 soft too, fuck it."

Angel walked back into the kitchen. "Alicia said she'll keep Angelica if you promise to bring her something from Houston."

"Give her some money and tell her I got her." He kissed her lips. "Meet me at the house in an hour. I need to make a quick run. Aye brah, that package will be at the spot for you. Give that to Lil Mane for me."

I fixed a plate of chicken, butter rolls, and mac and cheese. "You got the hang of the housewife role."

"Boy please, don't act like I wasn't cooking before I got with Jeremy. Anyway, I hear you got a cougar."

"Yeah, Toya hooked me up with her home girl Tammy."

She turned her nose up. "You know Jeremy fucked Toya. That was his payback for Buck fuckin' Dominique in August fuckin' you. Hmp, he fucked Xaviera too."

"You need a life." I laughed.

"My man is my life. Somebody has to see and hear what he can't." She put a plate in the microwave. "Let ma know her food is in here. I have to meet my booh. Ooh, one more thing, why you ain't tell me y'all beefin' with Crim?"

"It ain't nothing serious."

She grabbed her keys. "Oh. Okay, Bye."

"A'ight." I laughed at the thought of how nosey Angel was. "Lil brah ain't got a clue. Lil momma ain't missin' shit."

Chapter 2
Buck
"THE WARNING SHOTS"

Three days later

"Daddy, you need anything else before I leave?" I let her know I was cool.

August sat on the bed and kissed my cheek.

"Take Bria over to Sade's," I replied. She said she would, and then let me know Toya called while I was asleep.

"I'll be back in a couple of hours," she said as she left.

It had been three months since my accident. I'd been shot three times- once in the thigh, once in the hip, and once in the leg. Not only did I suffer from those injuries, but I'd broken two ribs, my left arm, and I fractured my pelvis. Yeah, I was fucked up, barely able to walk.

Like most days I was on bed rest, but it was Tuesday, and a little after 2 p.m. I had to call

Cappie.

"Cappie Lloyd's office, this is Stephanie."

"Steph, this is Buck Davis, is Cappie in?"

"Just a minute Bad Boy," she quickly replied.

I channel surfed while I waited for Cappie. After a couple of minutes he came on the line. "What's up?" he asked.

"I was making sure you remembered to call Edison."

"Everything set. Are you doing any better?" he asked.

I glanced at the cast on my leg and the one on my arm. "I tried to fuck my wife last night and my pelvis hurt so bad I couldn't stay hard."

"Damn, that's crazy. Have you decided how to handle that situation?" "Like a gangster. Anyway, I'll be in touch." I hung up, and then carefully climbed out of bed and into my wheelchair.

Since my injury, I relied on the wheelchair more than I was comfortable with, but my pelvis wasn't strong enough to support my weight. I wheeled myself to the kitchen to grab a snack. The phone rang – it was my homeboy Hoover Duke.

"Aye Groove, Criminal got merked on *The K.*" "When?" I asked. "Bout forty-five minutes ago. Like seventeen people got hit, over two hundred shots were fired."

I closed the cabinet and opened my cashews. "Aye Duke, I'll call you back."

"That's west up HCG LOC."

I dialed Tammy's number, Criminal was her uncle. She was distraught when she answered. She started explaining as soon as I asked her what happened.

"Five dudes jumped out of a blue Ford Explorer and started shooting."

I quickly processed the info, but knowing that Jinx and Criminal had a fist fight two days prior, I'd already put it together.

"Where are you?" I asked Tammy.

"I'm at home with Hurk. He was with me when I saw the news." "Aye, let me talk to him." I waited til Hurk got on the line. "Call your boy," I commanded.

He clicked over and called Jinx. "Hello," Angel answered.

Hurk asked to speak to Jinx. "Hold on, he just walked in dressed like Snoop Dogg with his black Dickies set and Chucks on," Angel replied.

Bingo! I thought to myself.

"What up Hurk?" Jinx asked.

Hurk asked if he'd seen the news or heard what happened. To which Jinx replied, "Niggas die every day, fuck um. If you didn't pull me off of him the other day, I would've beat him to death."

"Brah, tell me you've been with Angel." Hurk obviously thought the same thing I did.

Jinx laughed. "I've been with Lil Mane even if I wasn't, nothing seen, nothing said. Don't trip, you can let that handicap ass Buck know it wasn't me. But on Angelica, I ain't hiding from nothing or nobody. Anyway, I gotta go." He hung up.

"OG, let me see what's up," Hurk said.

"You have til the funeral. After that, I'm getting my people involved. But, I'll make sure your sister and niece are safe."

"Okay," was his simple reply.

Chapter 3
Jinx
"THE ALLURE"

I stepped on my front porch and watched the flow of traffic on my block. As always, Lil Mane and Val were right in the thick of it all – both posted on the curb.

"I'll call you when I get to the house," Staci said as she came out of the house with our one month old daughter. I carried Karma to Staci's Lexus truck and secured her inside of her car seat.

"Damn, I'm gonna catch hell with her," I said while admiring her beauty.

"Can I spend the night with y'all tonight?" I asked when I pulled Staci into my arms.

"Let me find out you like being around us." She kissed my lips. "Call when you're on your way. We love you."

"I love y'all too."

Lil Mane spoke to Staci as he joined me in the driveway. "Me and Val bout to ride to Walmart. Ace g'on handle the block til we get back."

"I'll be gone when y'all get back. I want you to call a meeting for tomorrow. Them niggas off Hoover 'posed to be tryna to sneak us."

He laughed. "I'm already on it." He showed me love, and then ran out to his Caprice.

I locked my house up, then got in my Cadillac truck and left. It was still fairly early – only 1:30 p.m. but all my guys were college boys so I was solo. Angel was at work and August was mad at me because I let Staci spend the night with me.

I decided to go to the mall when I received a call from Toya. She was leaving her office and called to ask if I'd meet her at a motel a couple of blocks away. Naturally, I agreed, making a U-turn and changing my destination.

As I headed to meet her, I couldn't help but think back to the first time she let me hit. She'd called me out the blue and told me she was on her way to my house. She got there in a trench coat, a gold bra and panties set, and six inch stilettos. From the second she entered my house until the moment she left, I tried to stamp my name on her body! That was three months ago, and since then I'd fucked her at least once a week.

"What took you so long?" she asked when I finally arrived at the room. She greeted me with a tongue kiss, and then let me inside, sitting me in a chair.

I noticed she grabbed a blindfold and a pair of handcuffs.

"What's up with this?" I asked, not trusting the set up.

"I want you to trust me. I have a surprise, but you can't see it or touch it. Well, not with your hands. If you agree, I'll promise you this will be the best you've ever had."

"I'll do the cuffs, but not the blindfold." I ran my fingers up her thighs, raising her skirt to reveal her purple panties.

She kissed my nose. "This is my show today."

"Do you then," I said.

She slipped a silk blindfold over my eyes, then cuffed my wrist together. She directed me to the bed, and then removed my shoes, socks, and pants. I felt her hands squeezing and stroking me to full attention, and then I felt another set of hands on my face.

"Shhh. Just relax," Toya whispered in my ear while the other chick went down on me.

"Jinx, you should see this bitch with her big pink ass lips wrapped around your dick. It feels good too, huh?"

"Who is that?" I asked.

She kissed my mouth and then straddled my face so I could lick her wetness which I was eager to do. Seconds later, I felt a condom being rolled down my shaft before I was eased into a tight wet slit.

"Oh my god, his dick is so big Toya." Cutie Pie's deep voice gave away her identity. "Fuck! I'm cumming already." She rode me so hard that the mattress started to squeak.

At the same time, Toya's juices flowed, drenching my face. "Yes! Oh god yes! Fuck me Jinx! That's it baby."

I was thrusting upward into Cutie Pie, matching her movements and bringing her to a body shaking climax. I don't know if she fell or climbed off of me, but I knew Toya pulled the rubber off and put another one on me.

"Was it good?" she whispered as she slowly eased me inside of her body. She rested her chest on top of mine and kissed my lips while slowly working her hips. She removed my blindfold but not the cuffs. Cutie Pie was on her knees behind Toya with a dildo in her hands.

"Y'all some cold freaks," I laughed when Cutie licked Toya's ass, then my nuts.

"I thought that's what you liked?" she asked. "Mmm... Boy, I wish I could clone this dick and take it with me. Oh well, I guess I'll just put this pussy on you til you can't get it back up," Toya moaned with a smile

Jinx
"EYEWITNESS"

It was after 6 p.m. when I finally left the motel. I did manage to put my dick in every hole Toya and Cutie Pie had though. Come to find out, it was Cutie Pie's 35th birthday and Toya gave me to her as a gift.

After I left them, I went to my house in Castalia to shower and change clothes. I then went and got Angelica from her mom. She was getting ready to go see the male dancers at *The Honeycomb*. I gave her some money to blow and then I left and went to Staci's.

"Staci, you're in here snoring and farting, smelling like a wild hog."

She laughed as she opened her eyes. "Ugh. That's your baby. Here, you change her."

"Look Angelica, you see your baby sister?" I let Angelica kiss Karma before I changed her shitty pamper. I took a few pictures of my daughters and sent them to my mom and my sister.

"It amazes me how good you are with them." Staci played with my twists. "I'm so glad I had a girl."

I pulled her down onto the bed. "Next time it'll be a boy." "No sir. One is enough for me. I'm made up like a *Magic City* stripper. Another baby and

I'll never get my Coke bottle shape back."

I kissed her while she held Karma. "I'll love you regardless. You know that, right?"

"I know. I just hate we didn't work out."

"You givin' up?"

"I'm a realist. You're married to the game and we both know Angel is the mistress. I'm just glad I got this out of the deal."

My phone rang. "Yeah, who's this?"

"Meet me at our spot," Vago said.

"I'm with Staci and my kids."

He spoke in Spanish, letting me know one of his spots had been robbed and three of his cousins killed.

"I'm on my way. I hung up and sighed in frustration. "I gotta make a run."

Staci was fixing Angelica a bowl of ice cream and Karma a bottle. "One of your whores?"

"N'all, that was Vago. Something happened."

"Be careful. Call me when you can." She held Karma up to me. "Kiss your baby." I

kissed my daughters, then Staci.

"You know I love you."

"Umm-Hmm. But you love your life more. I'll wait up. Tell your daddy bye Angelica."

"Bye-bye daddy! See you later."

I rushed out to my truck, calling Lil Mane as soon as I pulled off. "Aye, I need you to find out who hit a big lick. I need that info ASAP too."

Chapter 4
Jinx
"THE ART OF SEDUCTION"

"I'm sitting in the car."

"Get out and come in, my friend Britney wants to meet you."

I watched as the rain fell from the smoke colored sky. It was just past noon, but looked more like midnight. There wasn't a trace of blue anywhere in the sky, a far different scene from when I left my house. Fresh as I was, I wasn't about to get wet or muddy.

The front door opened and Tameka walked out to my car. She had a huge umbrella in her hand and a sexy smile on her face. I got out and held umbrella as the two of us made our way towards her house. When we got inside, the first thing I did was brush the water off my sneakers.

"You are a real pretty boy thug," Tameka commented. She smiled and kissed my cheek.

The two of us had been kicking it more and more over the past couple of months, even though her hating ass brother been dropping salt on me the entire time.

"I'm a Dinner Thief." I followed her into the den.

"Jinx, that's Lil Bit." Meka sat on the couch with me and held my hand. "This is the one I was telling you about," she said.

Lil Bit was sexy, a petite chick with wide hips and a round ass. I'd seen her before, but I couldn't recall where.

She smiled and waved. "You know Terio Speed and Jake?" she asked.

"Yeah, I put brah 'nem down."

"I know... I met you and Lucky at *JC's.* Y'all had that girl Birdie with you that night."

I suddenly remembered. "You had red hair." I watched as Tameka headed to her bedroom. I sat on the floor. "Yeah, you had on that Indian costume, got an angel or a fairy in the middle of your back."

She bit her lip, trying not to smile too hard. "It's a fairy, her name's Little Bit."

"Lil Bit, I want you to line his hair when I'm done twisting it down." Meka sat behind me and started taking my hair down.

"Your hair grows too fast. I could hardly grip it the first time I twisted it. Anyway, Lil Bit wanted to buy some weed."

I glanced over at shawty, and said, "You can't talk?"

"I didn't tell her to ask you that."

"Is it still raining?"

"A little. Why?" she asked.

I told Meka to give Lil Bit my keys. "Get that black backpack off the back seat and get the cigars from the console."

Meka pinched my arm as soon as her friend left.

"You fucked her," she said.

"How you figure that?" I laughed as I emptied my pockets, putting my money, phone, and my pistol on the table. "I ain't hit because Lucky was trying to. Plus she was scared. I spent about $6500 on her though."

"Whatever! Anyway, I told my brother about us."

"Fuck your brother," I replied honestly.

Lil Bit walked in with my bag. "Ooh, I love your car! That's a Trans Am? Champagne and blue. The night at the club, you were in a burnt orange Lexus." She gave me the bag and sat in the recliner.

"I just got the T.A. bout 2 weeks ago. I'm gettin' the Lexus painted honey gold."

Meka kissed my face. "My booh gettin' paper," she bragged.

"I see. Shit, he needs to put us on," Lil Bit replied.

I smiled at how forward shawty was. It was obvious that she had some hoodrat in her. I got up and emptied the pound of dro from my bag and onto the coffee table.

"Get them sandwich bags," I told Tameka. I tossed my shirt on Lil Bit's head, then lit one of the pre-rolled blunts I had in the cigar box. "Where you from?" I asked her.

“East Memphis, right off of Kirby Parkway. I ran away at 16. That’s when I started dancing. I used to mess with Sleepy, from Winchester Square.”

I passed her the blunt and then cut the bag open. The loud weed smell filled the room. When Tameka brought me the sandwich bags and the digital scale, I noticed that she'd changed clothes.

“Damn bitch, let me find out you're insecure. You went and put on your pussy print shorts and a t-shirt”" Lil bit passed Meka the blunt while teasing her.

I smacked Meka's ass, then pulled her into my lap when I sat on the couch. “I love her lil pussy print. Shit, I still ain't forgot how fat your gap was.”

“Shut up. My gap is not fat,” Lil Bit laughed.

“You in here flirtin' like you wanna suck his dick,” Meka said to her friend.

“Y’all chill out,” I said as I weighed the weed. “It's cool,” Lil Bit said. She smiled as Meka put her hand in my jeans.

“Keep playin',” she smiled.

Tameka stroked me inside my jeans, looking Lil Bit directly in her eyes.

“You wanna see it don't you. I'll suck it right in front of you.” I laughed so hard I wasted some of the weed. “Y’all two trippin'.”

Lil bit smiled. “Now you like dick again. Last night you tried to suck my clit off,” she rolled her eyes.

“Well, that was last night. Right now, I want you to come help me suck all this.”

Meka pulled my dick out, looked Lil Bit square in her eyes and put the first inch inside her mouth.

“Jinx, Lil Bit ain't never had no good dick and she wants to be a Jewel.”

“Oh yeah! Shit, why y’all ain't just say so. Put this shit up and meet me in the bedroom.”

Bounce

"SNAP-N-POP"

When I turned my bike into the lot of *Cutie Pie's* I pulled onto the sidewalk and hit the gas a couple of times. I came to the shop to drop off some money for Smurf. Since the day we started back dating, our relationship had quickly become serious.

Cutie Pie's was packed! It was Thursday, ladies' night at the club and Trey Songz was in town so the bad chicks were getting sexy for the show.

"Ugh, it's a two legged rat," Val joked. I hugged the home girl.

"What's up?" I spoke to all the other females in the lobby.

"You just missed Lucky and Hurk," Angel said. "My baby should be in the hood."

"Where's Smurf?" I asked her.

"Upstairs getting her nails done. Your baby momma is in the back," she whispered.

"Tell Smurf to meet me next door."

Before I could exit, Catera came from the shampoo area. "Angel said you came to surprise me," she said with a smile.

"Yeah, she told me you were here." I gave Catera some money for her hair and nails.

Smurf came into the lobby, rolling her eyes when she saw my baby's mom hugging me. I let Catera know I'd be with Jinx, and then I headed out to my bike.

Before I could pull off I got a call from Smurf. "I don't appreciate that," she whispered.

"I know. Come by Jinx's when you leave here, I'll make it up to you," I assured her.

After she agreed, I got on my bike and spanked off. When I get to the hood, Jinx and Icky were sitting on the porch listening to Yo Gotti, smoking weed, and watching the girls across the street wash their Navigator and Camaro.

“That bitch a dyke, the one built like Serena Williams. The light skinned one is fucking Lil Mane, the tall one let Yellow Boy hit.” Jinx showed me love. “You know you g’on have to fuck Cutie. If you don't she'll tell Catera about Smurf.”

I sat between him and Icky. “Catera can't stand Cutie. Anyway, what y’all got going?

“This fool talking about how many mixtapes he sold. Braggin' about the *Bet Hip-Hop Awards*.”

Icky looked at Jinx. “$750,000 advance from LA Reid. 375,000 mu'fuckin' mix tapes in 3 months.” He did a couple of lines of coke, and then offered me some. “Oh, you scared he g’on say something,” he said to me, referring to Jinx

“I ain't did no powder in two months.” I laughed, hoping he'd drop the conversation. If you've never snorted coke you wouldn't understand. Icky had fishscale – grade A product. All it would take was for me to smell or see it too long and I'd help him finish it.

Jinx looked at me and laughed. “You lyin' too brah. Angel said she caught you and Hurk gettin' blowed last night. That's what y’all do, I can't say shit.” He read a text, and then showed us a few pictures he received.

“Who is that?”

“Doll Baby's lil sister and her little partner. I had a threesome with them today.”

I noticed a dark colored Ford as it drove by the house for the third time. Jinx noticed it too, moving his pistol from his hip to his lap.

“Slick, you strapped?”

“I got the choppa on the backseat of the Crown Vic.”

As soon as Icky stepped off the porch shots rang out. The Ford hit the block and the occupants shot at us too. Jinx and I scrambled and made our best efforts to get Icky out of the line of fire, but to no avail. His body danced and twisted to the rhythm of the bullets as they hit him.

“Slick...Slick... Look at me, G.” I cradled him in my arms.

Jinx jumped in his Trans Am and headed after the Ford.

Two of the girls from across the street ran and let me know the other chick was a nurse. They also called 911. "B-B... Bounce, don't let Cool see me like this brah. Make sure I look gangster in that casket," Icky cried.

"You are gangster. *D.T.G.* Slick Icky. Nigga you are Killer D and Cool's son. Dirty Derek's lil brother."

He smiled. "Yeah, that's what's up. Never get full." He took one final breath and then died in my arms.

Chapter 5
Hurk
"THE SILVERBACK"

One week later

"You feel like talking?" Tammy asked me.

I was sitting on the trunk of my car smoking a blunt. We just left Icky's funeral and we were at his mom's house. The service was so crowded that the police came to make sure nothing violent jumped off. There weren't any suspects in the murder, nor were there any known motives, so things in the city were tense.

"I'm straight," I told Tammy as she wrapped my arms around her.

She wiped the tears from my face. "I want you to know that I'm here for you. I care about you for real. But I don't want you to do anything that might affect your future, our future."

"I know."

Jinx pulled up in his Trans Am and got out. "What's up Tammy? Aye brah, you ready?"
"Yeah." I kissed Tammy and let her know I'd call her later and then I got in the car with

Jinx.

"Lucky's at my house, Bounce is on his way." He passed me a bottle of Rose. "Did you see the two detectives at the church?"

"I saw I-40," I replied. I answered my phone. "Yeah!"

"Don't make a bad situation worse," Buck said.

"What would you do?" I asked.

He sighed and then hung up without another word. I turned my phone off as I told Jinx what I thought really got Icky shot.

"You know Slick hit your people for ten bricks and fifty pounds. I heard they found out we got um a while back too."

"They would've told me. They would've asked me to deal with him – trust me it was them niggas from Castalia and Magnolia. Even if it wasn't, that's who I'm taking it out on."

"Let's go holla at them niggas then," I replied. "I'm moving as soon as I catch Gooch slippin'." He turned down Person and headed towards Castalia. I asked him where he was headed.

"I'm going to the Yellow Apartments, fuck waiting. Grab the choppa off the backseat."

I pulled the wool blanket from the back seat and got the assault rifle. I checked the clip, then locked and loaded. I understood what Jinx was thinking.

He made a right onto Castalia and drove towards the apartments where Nacho and Gooch got money.

I hung out of the window and let off shots as we drove by. People were running, ducking, and hiding as I shot up the projects. Jinx slammed on the brakes and got out of the car. He shot the windows and tires out of Gooch's 645.

"Brah, c'mon!" I yelled.

He got back in and smashed off. "Reload, we're going through The Mound too. One of them might've helped."

"Get there then," I said.

He navigated the back streets until we were on Semmes and headed towards the heart of Orange Mound– Park and Pendleton.

"Don't get out this time. You know we have to be on point," I said. Remembering what happened to Bad Boy a few months prior.

He pointed to an orange on orange Tahoe parked in front of the community center. I up'd the AK and sprayed as he drove by. I saw a few people fall down, but wasn't sure if I'd hit anyone. My adrenaline was pumping, even as Jinx drove to his spot in South Memphis. He parked in the garage and then put the guns in a duffel bag that he quickly stashed underneath his doghouse.

"Drop me off at Pasha and Cookie's," I said.

We got in the Escalade and he pulled off. His phone was ringing off the hook.

"What... N'all me and Hurk in my truck. Angel, what I just tell your nosey ass? I'm on my way. I love you too." He hung up. "Angel said her friend called about a shootout in Castalia." He pulled into Pasha and Cookie's driveway.

"Be careful," I said when I got out.

"I'm a straight up G. If I die I'm taking plenty with me. Never get full brah."

"Never get full," I replied.

Jinx

"ANGEL'S WINGS"

"Baby, wake up. Buck is on the porch." Angel pinched my nose until I opened my eyes.

"Go see what he wants because I don't like him or how he was looking at my ass."

I slowly got up and put my shoes on. When I made it to my den, Buck was standing on my porch.

"What's up?" I asked.

"You John Wayne now? Or you Billy the Kid?"

I looked at him like he'd lost his mind. "Who you talkin' to?"

"Fuck all that. I came to tell you, stay away from my daughter."

"Oh yeah? Make sure you tell her that."

He walked out to his truck and let the windows down. To my surprise, August was in the passenger's seat – she would not even look my way.

"I hope you and your partners are ready for what you've started." He pulled off without another word. I stood on the porch and smoked a blunt. I was debating on how to deal with Buck; should I take him as a threat or should I ignore him the way I usually did.

"Baby, Victoria is on the phone."

"What's up," I answered once Angel was back inside the house. "Them dudes in The Mound got a *"SOS"* on you. Did you?"

I cut her off before she could finish her question. "What you think? You know me like the back of your hand."

"Well, you know you're always welcome in my home. Will I see you this weekend?"

I stepped inside the house, locking the front door before I joined my daughter on the floor.

"Probably. I'm playing with Angelica right now, but I'll call you."

"Okay. I love you booh. Bye-bye."

I put my phone on the table and picked Angelica up. "You wanna take a trip for a few days?" I asked Angel.

She laughed. "I have school. Besides, if you're so gangster, why would you run or hide."

"I'm not running or hiding, I'm protecting y'all." I reclined on the couch with Angelica on my chest. Angel cuddled up next to me, her fingers twisting my hair, my hands squeezing her panty-less ass.

"Baby, you should just leave it alone. Keep on grinding and being a good daddy. You're making too many enemies." She pulled her skirt down to cover her naked behind.

"Fuck them suckers."

She pinched my chest after Angelica's bad ass repeated what I said. "We need those suckers. You're gettin' $25,000 on the regular, $30,000 in this drought. That's not just because of your product, that's mostly because of your reputation. The streets love you, they love all y'all. Icky's funeral showed that. I'm not burying you, Jeremy. Shit, my tuition is too much." She smiled.

I kissed both my girls. "Did you wire Staci that money?"

"$1500!" She acted like she had an attitude. "She did text a picture of Karma in a cute Laker girl uniform." She showed me the picture on her phone. "She has your nose and your eyes."

I held Angelica up and looked into her chestnut colored eyes. She had my eyes too. "I'm about ready for a son. What about you?"

"Boy please! My ass and titties are too big." She got up and twerked. "I do want a big eyed little boy."

"Shit, I love how you look." She took Angelica from me and headed to the bedroom. Ooh, Jeremy, somebody killed Playa Joe."

"Good! Sucker ass."

She punched my chest. "Stop sayin' shit like that. I'm not visiting you in jail."

"Bullshit. Besides, I didn't shoot his bitch ass. Now, put the TV on Bart Simpson."

"I'm going to pick up Alexis."

"I'll be at my house." I grabbed my keys, and then carried my daughter out to Angel's truck.

She checked to make sure my pistol was on my hip. “Shoot first. I'll handle the rest. I've lied for you before.”

“I love you. I'ma marry your sexy ass.” I gave her some money and kissed both her and Angelica.

After she pulled out of the carport, I got inside my Cadillac truck and left her house.

I had to meet Meka and Lil Bit. They were at Applebee's with a couple of their friends. I went in and spotted them near the rear of the restaurant.

Aisha spotted me first. I met her once before and she was cool too. “Hey Jeremy! I wish I could clone you boy!” she said. Their fat friend flirted.

“I should've met you first!” she added.

I simply smiled, asking Meka and Britney to join me outside for a moment. Tameka got up, but Lil Bit took her time. She threw her hips as she made her way out to my truck.

“What's your malfunction?” I asked her.

She rolled her eyes at me. “Don't worry about it.”

“Here booh. That’s from Tino. Tameka kissed me after she gave me $1850. I gave her $550 back.

“Go get a new purse. Here, pay for the tab in there too.” I gave her some more money, then let her know I wanted to talk to Lil Bit in private.

“I'll call you,” Tameka said.

Britney slammed the door when she got inside the truck. “Here.” She threw the money she owed me.

I grabbed her by the collar before I even realized it. “What's your fuckin' problem?”

“You shot my little cousin! she cried.

“What? Who is your cousin?” I asked.

“Tela, from Castalia. You shot him in his arm and his hand.”

I lit a blunt and passed it to her. “I ain't shoot him, I know that lil fool. He's cool, he runs with Joe Street-grew up in the Third.”

“Well, he said you and some dude road through The Yellow Apartments in your Trans Am.”

I laughed. “My T.A is on Cameron in the garage. I've been with Angel and Angelica all afternoon – since the funeral.” I gave her the money she threw at me. “Here, put this up for me. You want me to spend the night with you?”

"At my house?" she asked. I could tell she was a little bit shocked. "In your bed, under your blanket, in my boxers."

She passed me the blunt. "Okay but Kat and Isha-Boo are gonna to be there too. You think that's a good idea?" She laughed. "You know how we get down – just like you and your partners."

"You let them see your stamp?"

"Um-hmm. They're scared, but they want you to put them down too. Anyway, I'll call you when I get home."

I kissed her nose, then watched her head back inside.

"Later for that Jinx. It's straight g-shit right now. Gotta go thru The Mound, let a mu'fucker see I ain't hiding."

Chapter 6

Lucky

"BACKUP PLAN"

One week later

"What's up girl? You got your soccer mom set on. Where y'all been?" I kissed Nyla and Koby as I let them inside my house. She hung Koby's jacket inside the closet.

"I took Koby to a birthday party at *Incredible Pizza.* Anyway, how was Miami??

"I drove back. Hurk was too drunk, Bounce drives too fast, and Jinx didn't come."

She made my bed. "You heard about Wildcat? They found him in the trunk of his car."

I put the cash from my pocket into my shoebox. "The streets ain't friendly, that's why I spend all my free time with you and Pooh."

I put my glock in the top of my closet, and then tossed my Polo shirt into the dirty clothes hamper. "All I'm doing now is managing models."

"Have you talked to Jinx about what you and your daddy decided?" "N'all, but I told them you're pregnant."

She blushed as I held her in my arms. "So, we're having a baby." "Damn right. And at the end of the month you're moving in with me. I broke up with Tia for you, and I chose you and Koby over Slick."

Koby ran into the room and climbed on my bed. "I want some green

Jell-O."

"Handle that while I answer my phone." I checked the number and it was my sister calling for Jinx.

"Someone killed Youngblood while Jinx was with him."

I let Nyla know I had to leave. She asked me to stay, saying she had a funny feeling about something. I told her I'd call when I got to Jinx's and then I left. Twenty minutes later I was parking my Corvette in front of Jinx's. Him and Hurk were standing in the driveway. As soon as I got out I asked them what happened.

"Him and Ziggy shot each other. He got hit in the face; Ziggy got hit in the stomach." Jinx continued to text on his phone. "They thought Youngblood had some bogus dice, but he didn't." He looked at me. "Me and Lil Mane g'on to ride on them suckas."

"Youngblood ain't *DTG,*" I replied.

"That's Val's brother. Bounce is with her right now," he added.

"This nigga just trigger-happy," Hurk said in reference to Jinx.

Jinx received a text and suddenly started laughing. "Go home brah. Nyla called Staci. Matter of fact, y'all right, I'ma let it go." He sat on the trunk of his Lexus. "I'm finna get this last brick off."

"I'm out." I got in my car and spanked off. I wasn't about to deal with Jinx and his split personality.

I stopped at Night& Day corner store and got a box of cigars. I noticed an orange Caprice parked at the car wash across the street. "*H.C.G.*," the driver yelled and threw gang signs.

"Fuck! Them niggas from *Hoover*," I said, suddenly realizing the danger I was in. I was so nervous that I dropped my keys and the Chevy was headed my way! They opened fire but to my surprise, Jinx's Trans-Am sped towards them with Lil Mane returning fire.

"Get in!" Jinx yelled as he swerved in front of me. "Something told me to ride up here. They tried to get your goofy ass," he laughed.

"What's funny!" I yelled.

He laughed harder. "You pissed on yourself! Damn, I wish Slick was here. Aye brah, you can square up. You, Bounce, and Hurk. Me and my youngin' got them fools. Y'all g'on play house, it's all good. I know your daddy and your girl want you to leave me alone." He laughed harder. "I love you big brah. On Slick, I'll kill them fools for you."

Jinx

"GANGSTER,GANGSTERS"

"Aye brah, whose car is that?" Lil Mane pulled his gun from his pants and carefully watched the dark tinted, white Nissan Galant park in front of my spot.

My phone rang. "Yeah, what's up?"

"I'm outside your spot. Who is this? August?"

"Damn, you can't recognize my damn voice?"

I hung up on her, then Lil Mane to put his gun up as I made my way out to the car.

"Get in and stop playing!" August snapped.

I slowly got into the car, leaving the passenger side door open. "What you doing over here? I thought your daddy told you to stay away from me?"

She handed me a positive pregnancy test. "I haven't told him, but Toya knows. Oh, I know you fucked her too."

"How far along are you?" I asked.

"About a month and I want it," she said.

I couldn't contain my smile. "I'm glad. I hope it's a boy. It'll probably be another girl, knowing my luck. Anyway, what you gonna do about Buck?"

"I'm grown and if he can't respect that then oh well. I expect you to spoil my baby the same way you do Karma and Angelica."

I kissed her nose. "I promise you'll never have to worry about that. Anyway, how you figure I fucked Toya?"

"She told me when I told her I was pregnant. I can't be mad, I did fuck Hurk."

"It was never about that." I was being honest. "The reason I fucked

Toya was more about how fine she was and the fact I hate Buck!" I read a text from Val letting me know she was on her way to the spot.

"Can I take you to lunch tomorrow?" August asked.

"What time?"

"One. Come over here when you get out of class." I kissed her lips. "I can't wait to see what we look like."

She smiled. "I'll see you tomorrow. Be safe."

"A'ight." I got out of the car and stood on the curb while she pulled off.

"Who was that?" Lil Mane asked.

"August. We gotta end this lil shit with Gooch. G'on to get rid of his punk ass. Anyway, roll a blunt, Val should be here in a minute. I want to use some more of these bullets and guns we bought, ya dig!"

Chapter 7
Bounce
"THE RESCUE"

"I talked to Buck this morning. He wants to sit down with you and Hurk." My sister handed me a bowl of gumbo, then sat at the table with me. "You should at least listen."

"For what? He already accused us of crossing him. He told Hurk he should've killed Jinx. How that look, me choosing to him over Jinx?"

"All I'm asking is that you talk to your nephew's dad. Whether you realize it or not, this is affecting Zion and me too."

I was listening, but she was full of shit! If she wasn't still in love with Buck she would see my point.

"I'll see," I replied.

"You know what, fuck it do what you wanna do. I'm tryna to help you stay out of the Feds, cause that's where Jinx is headed."

I put my bowl in the sink, washed my hands, then headed to the front door. I ignored her yelling my name. I needed to leave to avoid hurting her feelings. I got in my Corvette and left. I hated being mad at her, but when it came to Buck she was too crazy in love to listen to me. My guys were in Cummings Park. Some guys tried to gun Lucky down the day before, so the OG's in the city wanted to have a peaceful resolution. They knew Jinx and his youngsters thrived on bullshit!

To my surprise, Buck and Hoover Duke were there. I greeted them, and then joined my guys.

"Brah, they think we killed Crim," Jinx said.

"Why? He was a'ight with me." I sat on the car with Jinx. "You believe that?" I asked. "Mane, fuck that. I say that we just make them drop this Dinner Thief shit. They on some renegade shit," Hoover Duke said..

"This ain't that," Hurk said.

"Fuck this shit. If a motherfucker got a problem it's whatever!" Jinx said as he stood up.

"I'm on Lapolma everyday. If I ain't there, I'm on Cameron. Whoever got a problem can come see me."

A few of the older cats laughed and whispered amongst themselves. I was noticing the facial expressions and body language. They were mad. But Jinx had their attention and respect.

"Jinx, you can't make threats," one of the elder cats said.

Jinx laughed. "If a mu'fucker don't like it they can act on it. It won't be the first time. We been at war since we started *D.T.G.* Niggas feel like we owe 'um something."

He looked at each of them. "We respect who respects us... When Fish started *Memphis Mob* he had to earn respect. Train earned it when he started *LMG*- he died for it too! When Wiz started the *Y.D.4.L.* He earned it. That's all we're doing. What niggas mad for? Cause we ain't kissin' ass? Cause we ain't gotta go thru them to get money?"

He pointed at each of us. "We ain't payin' no taxes, we ain't answerin' to no Committee of Thugs, and if it's a problem we got guns and soldiers too."

"Jinx, chill out," I said.

Hurk got in the car with Jinx. "When we find out killed Icky, we'll chill out," he said.

"Did you talk to your sister?" Buck asked.

"I made my choice. I'm a *Dinner Thief* til I die."

Chapter 8
Buck
"PREPARATION"

"Have you heard from your boys since the other day?" My wife handed me a plate of fried catfish and spaghetti then joined me on the couch.

I never took my eyes off the TV, so she turned it off. "Buck Davis, don't get slapped!" she said.

"You ain't talkin' bout shit. Fuck them lil dudes."

August walked in and sat in the recliner. "Daddy, can I go to San Juan, Puerto Rico? London has a photo shoot next weekend."

"We'll see," I replied.

"All you have to say is yes or no," she said matter-of-factly.

"August, don't you have something to tell your daddy?"

I glanced at Toya, then August. I knew what it was. "Please, not by him."

"Yep. Seven weeks and Jeremy is so excited. And if you think he killed Criminal, he didn't because I was with him."

I told her to call Jinx. She did, but Angel answered his phone.

"Angel, this is Buck, is your boy around?"

"My man is in Castalia. Anyway, congratulations on the grandchild, I guess we're family now. I hope August has a healthy baby, but she can't have *my man*."

"I understand. Anyway, have a good day."

I gave August her phone, then made my way out to my truck. I instructed my daughter not to leave before I got back. I had to find Jinx!

It took me almost an hour to track him down. When I did, he was with Lil Mane and three females. The five of them were having lunch at *A&R Barbeque*. He spotted my truck in the parking lot, and then made his way outside.

"What did I tell you about my daughter?" He checked a text on his phone.

"You should've told her. I'm grown so is she."

"That cocky shit doesn't impress me," I said.

He smiled. "Let's be honest. You don't like me, I don't like you. But if you respect me, I'll do the same. I mean, at least try for August's sake."

"There won't be any second chances."

I got in my truck and peeled off. I had to make another stop not far from where I was.

I pulled up on Gooch and Nacho in front of Mangolia Elementary School. It was amazing. They were beefing with Jinx, yet he hustled from a street two minutes away.

"What's up Bad Boy?" Nacho gave me dap.

"Y'all can't touch Jinx."

Gooch laughed. "Why not?"

"I'll handle him." I looked them both in the eyes just to stress how serious I was. "I'll be in touch" I got in the truck and dialed I-40's number as I pulled off.

"Que Pasa," he answered.

"It's me. Cut his water off," I said sternly. "Collect and cash him out. I have two guys better suited. I'll call you in a couple of days for a meeting."

I hung up. *There's more than one way to skin a cat. It's time Jinx learn who really runs the city Bad Boy Buck Davis*, I said to myself.

Chapter 9
Jinx
"DINNER THIEF GANGSTER"

Two weeks later

I stood on the porch in front of my spot on Cameron and watched the happenings on the block. The little young cats were chasing cars for drug sales, the girls were out in their hoochie gear, and the kids were having a water fight. It was a typical Spring in South Memphis and I was in a good mood!

Vago and I-40 told me that Buck wanted them to cut off their dealings with me. The three of us came to an understanding, Buck Davis couldn't control anything we did, especially not our business! We did make one change. Instead of 40 bricks a month, I would get 50 – that was their way of showing their appreciation for my loyalty.

A purple Acura pulled up and parked across the street. Kat and Lil Bit got out and walked up the hill to the porch.

"Ooh, don't you look like a ball player in your throwback Magic Johnson jersey and gold Chucks on." Lil Bit hugged me and kissed the corner of my mouth. The three of us went into the house.

She started cleaning up as soon as she walked in. "Ugh. I hate coming over here on the weekends. You need a maid."

"He has you," Lil Bit replied. She sat on the couch and turned the TV on.

"You always have an attitude," I said as I rested my head in her lap, smiling while she played with my hands. “Did you do what I asked you to do?” I asked her.

She twisted my hair. “This morning. And I have an attitude because you didn't do what you promised.”

“I had to meet my people. But, y’all can keep me company tonight,” I said.

“Ooh, Jeremy I want you to take me to the movies next weekend.” Kat sat on the couch and pulled me into her lap.

“It'll have to be Friday because I'll be in Chicago Saturday and Sunday. I want y’all to stay here next weekend,” I added.

Lil Bit closed the front door and locked it. She kicked off her heels as she rested her petite frame on top of my body. She reached inside my pants and pulled my pistol out, placing it on the table.”

“I'm dancing all next weekend,” she said after kissing my lips.

Kat's dress had inched its way upward, revealing her bare and shaved vagina. Her lips were big with a real camel toe!

“Damn Kat. Your pussy is so fat. No wonder that nigga Eric can’t handle you!” I said.

“I told her the same thing. This bitch has a 10 inch dildo under her bed!” Lil Bit added.

Kat put my hand underneath her dress. “You feel how wet you make me?” She put my fingers into her opening, then took them out, and put them in a Lil Bit’s mouth.

My phone started ringing and interrupted the moment. “Hello.” I answered my phone only because it was Angel's number. She was hysterical and she told me to get to the hospital asap. Bounce was in the ER. He flipped off his bike and was run over by a car.

I rushed out of the house and left so quickly, I didn't even tell my girls what was up. When I got to the emergency room, Angel was waiting out front with Hurk. I could tell by their body language that the worst was a reality.

“He's gone Lil Brah.” Hurk shed a few tears as he embraced me.

My knees get weak and I fell to the ground. “He got side swiped by a red Mustang. He beat up Gooch earlier. Smurf said Gooch might've sent somebody at brah,” Hurk informed me.

I regained my composure, holding Angel and she cried. “Why didn't I know about Gooch?”

"They were at Val's." Hurk rubbed his chin, our signal to speak in code. "You think she knew about South Padre?"

I thought momentarily, remembering Bounce and Lucky had robbed Gooch a few months ago. Val knew because she was messing with Gooch at the time. Afterwards, Lucky, Bounce, Tia, and Val went to South Padre Island in Texas as an alibi.

"She knew, but she ain't no rat or traitor. Val is family, a real gangster."

I rubbed my chin.

"Stop giving him signals and shit!" Angel snapped. "Y'all need to end this shit because I'm not burying either of you. Now let's go check on Zandria, Zion, Catera, and Smurf."

"I gotta go."

Angel grabbed my arm. "No, you need to go see them."

"I need to do what you said." I kissed her lips, promising to call her in an hour. Only then did she let me leave.

My mind was racing 100 miles per hour. Gooch was the type to retaliate if given a reason and if Lucky and Bounce robbed him he had a reason. I had to go see him because if he killed Bounce he was next to die!

It shocked him when I walked into the community center where he hung out. I caught him and Nacho shooting pool.

"Damn. Fuck you doing here?" he smiled as he racked the balls.

I grabbed the stick and hit the cue ball and broke the other fifteen up. "Real gangsters go where the wind blows. Shit, it's quiet on this side of the tracks. On my side we got a heavy dose of traffic."

"You just started gettin' money, but nobody respects a thief," he replied.

I smiled at Nacho and Gooch laughed. "Nigga fuck you and your respect. You're a used to be, was nigga. I'll buy your trick ass. Two bricks will get you and this bitch put in a box. A Dodge Charger might get you gang raped."

He stepped in my face. "You ain't untouchable. I'm not Crim or Murder Mook. And I ain't Buck either."

"If I find out you killed Bounce, it won't matter."

He smiled. "Now you're a killer?"

"N'all I'm a thief, I steal souls from pussy ass has beens." I put the pool stick on the table and walked out.

Just as I was about to get in my car, a blood red Mustang 5.0 pulled up. Two young cats got out. They noticed me and both had a look of terror on their faces. They ran in opposite directions. I got in my car and sped off in high pursuit.

Docka! Docka! Docka! Docka! Docka! Docka!

I shot out of the window as I got closer. I knew all the cuts and pathways so I tried to guess where they might be headed.

"Fuck!" I saw them in my rearview, headed in the opposite direction. I turned around to see Gooch's Lexus was headed my way. He swerved and hit a light pole when I fired shots at his windshield. I just declared war on them and their crew. It was zero tolerance for all enemies and allies of my enemies!

I dialed Lil Bit's number and told her to clean out my spot in Castalia, then I called Lil Mane and ordered him to get all our soldiers together – it was time to go to battle!

Chapter 10
Lucky
"YOU ARE WHO YOU ARE"

Two weeks later

My phone had been ringing all day. Everyone was eager to hear about me and Nyla getting married in Vegas. This particular call was from Buck. He not only congratulated us, but also invited us to join him and Toya in Chicago for the grand opening of his nightclub. Naturally, I agreed, and let him know I'd have my wife call his wife. After my phone call I decided to head to the hood. Since finding out he was my dad, he and I grew closer. He took me under his wings and Toya did the same to Nyla, and they both adored her.

Since Bounce died, I hadn't hung out much. The streets were too crazy – not only with our beef, but *The Wolfpack* was going at the *Playa Posse*. On top of that, there was a drought on weed and coke – which made matters worse.

By the way Lil Mane's spot looked, something major was going on in the hood.

"Fuck y'all got going on?" I asked Hurk as I walked up on him and Jinx.

They were seated on the trunk of Jinx's 82 Cutlass. The car matched Jinx's North Carolina shorts and Jordan's – he didn't have on a shirt, but he had on more jewelry than a rapper shooting a video!

Jinx passed me the blunt he was smoking. "I put the whole hood down this morning. I'm tryna put the whole damn town down.. South Memphis,

East Memphis, North Memphis, and The Haven. It’s Dinner Thieves takeover.”

“What's up with him?” I asked Hurk about Jinx.

He laughed as Jinx stood on top of his Trans Am – which was also parked on the curb. “He said something about a takeover, a movement. He's been like this since yesterday.

Fuck that, you married and shit?”

“Yeah, I had to wife shawty, brah. Anyway, back to Lil Brah.”

“Angel called me yesterday and said Jinx was in a good mood. When I got with him he was full of Kush, doing exactly what he's doing now. He got ten bricks in the house, about two hundred pounds of weed. That fool been turnt up since I've been here!”

“Aye Hurk, the price of good pussy finna go through the roof! All these niggas screamin’ $17,500... Mr. 17.5- a mu'fucker can't get half a brick for that! Not unless he’s a *Dinner Thief*,” Jinx bounced around like a boxer, grooving to Migos “Bad & Boujee.”

“I thought the Mexicans cut his water off?” I said to Hurk.

He looked at me. “Ain't no way brah. Jinx buyin' what they used to front him. That fool don' murked people for them. They love him like family for real! That’s 5 bricks on his wrist, 7 on his neck! That fool workin' with a million!” he said proudly.

“Get the fuck out here!” I said in disbelief.

Jinx punched me in my chest. “Congratulations brah on the wedding and the modeling contract. I'm happy for you. Y’all make sure when they do my documentary that they keep it trill.”

He pointed to the honey colored Lexus that had just turned the corner. “My youngin' comin to check in.”

“Angel know you got another broad pushin' the Lexus?”

“Aye Lucky, I'm not you brah. Angel is going to Jamaica next week. She don't give a damn about that shit you talkin' about.”

He walked out to the car, and Hurk laughed. “He’s only 19! We used to have to watch his every move... Now he has all these people doing it for him.”

“We grew up. It's his turn now,” I replied honestly.

Hurk

"STRONGER AND WISER"

"I'm bout to take Catera some money. Bounce left a lil something for her, but I'll make sure she's good too-her and the baby," Jinx stretched then grabbed his keys.

The two of us stepped out onto the porch. "I need to go by my mom's, and then I'll be with Tammy. I'll call you in the morning," I told him.

I got in my car and drove to my mom's. All four of my sisters were in the kitchen cooking and talking about the latest episode of *Love and Hip-Hop*. Amy met me at the door with a hug and a kiss. I greeted each of my sisters, then asked Alicia what they were up to.

She let me know they were making my mom a birthday dinner and a cake.

"Which one of those girls was driving my baby's car?" Angel asked.

Alexis laughed. "Britney Wade. She had Isha-Boo with her too."

"The stripper? What they call her, Lil Bit? Hmp, I figured it was the white girl," Angel replied.

"Kat is Armanian, like Kim Kardashian. She has a baby by that fine ass Eric Moy!"

"Alexis, how you know them?" Alicia asked.

"They went to White Station with my boyfriend. I've known them since 7th grade. It's Isha-Boo, Meka, Kat, Lil Bit, and Tay Tay."

"Meka is Doll Baby's sister. Her lil ass was messing with Jeremy at first." Angel smiled when Jinx walked in carrying their daughter.

"I thought you had to go back to Catera's?"

He kissed her lips. "I picked up Angelica from my mom's. You're spending the night with me." He tossed her his keys. "C'mon because

Catera is waiting."

"You can't just order my big sister around," Alexis said.

He gave her some money. "You're keeping Angelica tomorrow," he said.

Him, Angel, and Angelica left. I ate then headed out to Tammy's.

When I got there she was asleep on the couch, holding the teddy bear I'd given her for our six-month anniversary. The sight of her, along with all I was feeling – Lucky's marriage, Icky and Bounce dying, Jinx's crash course to the pen – had me reflecting on my future. I knew what I wanted!

I dialed Jinx's number. "I called to let you know I'm always eating at the table, but your plate is your plate, ya dig"

He was silent momentarily. Then he said, "Just don't get full big brah."
"Never brah." I hung up then joined my lady on the couch. I held Tammy and the thought

about Lucky's words. We had grown up, now it's was Jinx's turn.

Chapter 11
Buck
"THE POINT OF ATTACK"

Three months later

"Forget that club. First it was a shootout, then a fight, now it's a fire. I should've opened a beauty salon." Toya laughed as she continued to shave me head. "We should move to Florida or Arizona. I'm ready to just lay back and enjoy what we have. I mean, you've beat the Feds once."

"I didn't beat um, I gave um 10 and some change."

"But you could've had a life sentence. I could've been your co-defendant," she said honestly.

I didn't respond, knowing she was exactly right.

"You know, I used to thank God every day for letting you and BoBo get away. It was crazy cause all Romeo had to do was shut up and he would've walked."

"Well, I'm glad we're done with that. You're a grandpa now. Speaking of which! You know August talked to Jeremy?"

I didn't say anything, but I knew all about Toya and Jinx creeping a few months prior. I'd actually known from the start, but refused to expose it because I knew I deserved it. She'd stayed by my side during my entire bid, how could I trip over anything she did?

"She thinks Ziggy told on him," she continued.

"He'll be a'ight." I kissed her lips after she wiped my freshly shaved head.

"I'll be back. I need to put some money BoBo's books."

"Be safe."

I left the house and went straight to Western Union. It had been a while since I been through Riverside so after I took care of my brother, I stopped on Kansas Street.

I spent a couple of hours on *The K* with the homeboys- smoking and drinking- then I headed home. It was 9 p.m. when I got there. I was high and a little drunk, but I was on point.

"Fuck all these lights out for?" I got out and made my way up the driveway. Just as I reached my wife's car I noticed her keys on the ground.

I got my snub-nose .38 from my ankle holster and carefully checked out the scene. There were three guys in my living room. My wife was naked and tied to a chair. My daughter Bria and baby Brian were tied up too, seated on the couch. "Shit!"

I took a deep breath and prepared to save my family. I crept to my truck and put a brick on the gas pedal. I started the truck and put it in drive.

Boom!

It crashed into the tree near the front of my home. Thirty seconds later, two of the robbers came running out the front door.

"Ugh." I jumped from behind the bushes and snapped the first guy's neck, then used the body for a shield as the other guy fired at me.

"2 down, one to go," I said after I shot the other cat in his head and chest.

As I headed inside, I noticed 2 more cats. They shot at me as I made a break towards my backyard.

"Daddy!" Bria screamed. The guy from inside had her on my porch at gunpoint.

I recognized Gooch's voice as soon as he said, "Bad Boy, you can't win Cuzz. Cough that money up before I get mad." I could hear the police sirens in the distance. I had an idea- I stepped out of the darkness with my hands up.

"Leave them out of this."

"Fuck that. I'm taking them with me. I'll call you," he said as his guys walked my wife and kids to their getaway car.

As soon as he motioned to open the car, I pulled my other gun from my waistline and opened fire. I dropped him and one of the other two guys.

"Police… Put the gun down!"

"Wait... I'm the owner."

"Put the goddamn gun down!"

Just as I was about to drop my gun, I noticed a guy running from the rear of my home. Before I could move or speak, gunfire erupted. The last thing I heard was my wife's crying – that, and my own heartbeat.

Chapter 12
Jinx
"NOTHING SEEN, NOTHING SAID"

One month later

"Vaughn...Jeremy Vaughn, report to visitation." The fat white officer called me from the front of the dorm.

I'd been locked up for the past four weeks as part of a 16-person conspiracy. From what I knew, Vago and I-40 got indicted with Ziggy Zaggs. A mule gave them up and everyone else they served. Because I was being watched, the Feds were able to get all my people as well. The fact that I had a couple of prior drug charges, the DEA was eager to keep me in custody.

Other than myself, Ziggy, and the Esses, I was on the charge with Gangster Greg, Sleepy, Fatts, Vida, Mercedes, Sandman, and 6 of Vago's mules. Needless to say, but I was not feeling too comfortable. I was nervous but thankful Terio, Jake, and August were free.

I took a quick shower and put on my visitation set and a pair of tan and brown Gucci loafers, then I made my way to my visit. A feeling of pride filled my heart as I watched Angel and Angelica enter the small visitation room.

"That's your family?" one of the older cats asked.

"My shawty and our daughter. Oh snap, that's my mom too!"

I banged on the glass to get my mom's attention. I had not talked to her since I was arrested – I knew the results of my choices, she shouldn't have to defend me to Major Vaughn.

"Don't hit the glass inmate."

I looked the officer got up and down. "This chubby, Precious lookin' ass," I mumbled to myself.

"Vaughn, c'mon," the Lt. said.

I turned my swag on and made my way into the room they used for the strip searches. After a degrading process of getting naked in front of a man, I was allowed to enter the visiting room. Angelica stumbled towards me with a smile on her face.

"Hi daddy," she laughed.

"Who cut your hair?" Angel asked after a quick hug and a kiss. She ran her hand over my freshly faded hair.

"Fatts did it earlier," I said.

My mother hugged me with tears in her eyes. "You look so handsome-just like Major Vaughn!" she said proudly.

I sat down with my daughter in my lap and asked about my dad. My mom let me know he was concerned about me and that I should give him a call. I hated my dad prior going to prison, but as I matured, I realized his tough love was his way of trying to teach me how to be a man. I loved him and he loved me. We just hated the way the other lived.

"I might give him a call. Angel, get my lil mama some gummy bears," I said.

"I'll do it," my mom said. She took Angelica and headed toward the vending machines, leaving us alone.

"Damn Angel, you look so sexy! Who you been fuckin'?" I asked after kissing her again.

She pinched my nose. "That dildo you gave me. Anyway, are you alright"?

"I'm cool. Did you get that money I told you to collect?"

"I got nineteen stacks from Jake, ninety-five hundred from Terio, and your bitch brought $12,500 this morning."

I laughed. "Put five thousand on my books and the rest goes in your savings account. Tameka and Vicky g'on bring some money for you too, put that in Angelica's account."

She held my hands and listened carefully. It was now time to see if all my time, trust, and love would pay off. I knew she loved me, but could she love me at a distance?

"Did you get that other money?" I asked.

She smiled when our daughter climbed in my lap. I opened her candy and let her feed me a couple gummy bears. "She's spoiled rotten," Angel said proudly. "Anyway, there was money in Castalia and Cameron, and $143,220 at Lil Mane's- plus all that weed and cocaine!"

"Shhh... Stop talking so loud, these fools are nosey!" I laughed.

"I'm serious! I've counted over a million dollars in three damn days. That's not adding what's at my house or at your house, or what your lil hoes have put up."

I cleaned her Louis Vuitton glasses and looked into her hazel eyes. "Don't worry baby you've mastered your position. I want you to sell my car and my truck. Matter-of-fact,

call Fred Wooten and tell him to take care of it – he has a lil car lot."

My mom rejoined us. "How long are we going to deal with this? What did Zandria say? Oh, and do I have any more secret grandbabies?"

I laughed at her questions. "Zandria told me to be patient, but with my two misdemeanor charges and this forty thousand gram conspiracy, I'll get a least sixty months. I didn't get caught selling nothing, but somebody will testify if I try to go to trial. 5 years- that's like college ya dig."

"Boy shut up. Anyway, answer the other question," Angel said.

Angelica continued to feed me. "August is due in November. The baby's name is Malaysia Joi."

"Victoria's baby is due when?" Angel inquired.

"Victoria?"

"Yeah! It's all over Facebook and Twitter and The Gram!"

"I didn't know that. I will check her for that though."

Angel rolled her eyes and said, "I saw a ring I want, it's $93,000." She got up and walked to the microwave to warm up my hot wings. Her bowlegged ass looked too sexy in her pink high waist denim pants and stilettos!

"I love her! Your dad does too." My mom noticed the way I was watching Angel.

"Anyway, stay out of trouble, your dad is going to call in a few favors." She took Angelica from me. "I love you, but I have a date with my grandchild. Call me in a couple of days."

Angel hugged my mom, and then rejoined me after warming our food. "Now, back to my ring. Am I worth $93,000?"

"Stop playin', you know why I went so hard. All that Gucci, Louis V., Prada. The Red Bottoms, Badgley Misckas, Guisseppes. I love to see you in that shit, ya dig."

She flipped her thirty inch hair and smiled. "You know my momma moved with her man her, Amy, and Alicia – she's transferring to Georgetown. Alexis is moving in with me."

"That's cool. Staci's moving back to Memphis. She wants to be closer to me – so Karma can see me."

"I'm fine with that. Ooh, you know Lucky got Yellow Boy and Trevor a deal with Def Jam. And he got Ebony and Smurf some kind of modeling contract. And Buck is out of the ICU."

"August told me he's walking. His ass got hit nine times and had a stroke, now he's walking. If God ain't on his side I'm a dick eating dog!"

"You're stupid boy. Anyway, Lil Mane said something about the count is 495."

I smiled- the gang had doubled in the month I'd been gone!

"Lil Mane g'on call you once a week. Use what he gives you to handle your bills."

I fed her a wing. "Give him my Cutlass and all my clothes and jewelry. Ooh, get the money out the car before you give it to him."

"It was $75,000. I took half to August and half to Staci. Hmp, you know my brother and Tammy are getting married in December? I think she's pregnant. I wish I was having a wedding day and a baby."

The two of us waved at Star. She was visiting Gangsta Greg.

"Shhh. Patience shawty, this is only a setback. Keep the phone straight, put two hundred dollars a week on my books, and take care of Angelica. From now on, only use the money you've collected to take care of your business. What I told you to put in the bank is to save."

"Okay. Can I keep your Escalade though?"

"Yeah. And don't worry, you'll still be able to wear those $800 hooker heels and fly designer brands. Daddy was well prepared for this part of the game too. I was not playing out there- I had more bricks than the projects, and the streets owed me twice as much as you've counted!"

She smiled. "What about my panties? You know I can't have nothing cheap touching this pussy – that's what daddy told me."

"He taught you well. That's why he knows you'll be good. Now, no more talking, I just want to look at you til it's time to go."

We sat quietly for over an hour, until I finally spoke. “Angel! You know, when I marry you, you'll be a *Dinner Thief*?”

“I'm Jinx's Jewel.” She moved the hair from the right side of her neck to show the tattoo of my name inside the jewelry box.

“N’all, I'm talking some trill shit.” I laughed. “That's part of your vows.”

“Jeremy, I'm not stuntin’ you.”

I thumped her nose. “I'm dead serious. Repeat after me.”

“Ugh. You make me sick.”

“Nothing seen, nothing said. Loyalty is everything! We snatch all plates, but never get full.” She repeated my words, looking me in the eyes as she did.

“I love you Angel Monique. I can't wait to wife you and make our dreams come true.” After my visit I was again strip searched. On my way back to the dorm I passed the same old head I'd seen before my visit.

“Aye youngster, you know Jinx he got dreads and a lot of tattoos?”

I smiled. “I've heard about him.”

“Yeah? He must be important because them young boys in medical was talkin' bout him.”

The two of us headed to the dorm. “Say he like Tookie Williams or Larry Hoover, G-Train – started his own gang, him and his boys. Say he a millionaire too, ain’t but nineteen or twenty and he stood up to Buck Davis and them real OG's too. If he done that, he's the real deal!”

“What up Jinx,” Doll Baby said. He was in Mason for a bank robbery him and Murder Mook did.

I gave him dap. “Meet me in the gym, I gotta dude who want to play you 1-on-1 for $1000 a game – easy money, ya dig.”

“That’s cool.” He looked at the old head. “What's up Oz?” “Oz? You’re Wiz-Casper Reeves, from East Memphis? The Don of Dons?” I took a good look at my idol and smiled. “The River City Wizard!”

He smiled as we shook hands. “It's an honor to meet you Jinx.”

“You're a legend!” I said honestly.

“Yeah, you too! You, Icky, Bounce, Hurk, and Lucky. Don't get full yet, you have a lot more to eat, you feel me?”

I smiled. “I'll never get full, this is only making me that much hungrier.”

Book Order Form
Legit Styles Publishing
16501 Shady Grove Rd Suite #7562
Gaithersburg, MD 20898

Name: ____________________ Inmate ID: ______________
Address: ____
City/State: ____

QUANTITY	TITLES/AUTHORS	PRICE	TOTAL
	KINGPIN, Byron Grey	15.00	
	The Wall Season 1, Don Twan	15.00	
	Confessions of A Cheating Heart, Donnie Ru and Don Twan	15.00	
	No TrustPassing, Hood & Face 1	15.00	
	Pay The Cost, Michael "Blue" Branch	15.00	
	A.B.C.G. (Anybody Can Get it) DeSean Gardner	15.00	
	Small Town Cemetery DeSean Gardner	15.00	
	Dinner Thieves, Zo Ali	15.00	
	COMING SOON!!		
	KingPin 2, Byron Grey		
	The Wall 2, Don Twan		
	No TrustPassing 2, Hood and Face 1		
	The Initial Investigation, Byron Grey		
	Murderland, Byron Grey		

Sub Total $_______ Shipping $________ Total Enclosed $_________

Shipping & Handling (Via US media Mail) $ 3.95 1-2 book(s), $ 7.95 3-4 books, 4 books or more free shipping.

FORMS OF ACCEPTED PAYMENTS:

Certified or government issued checks and money orders, all mail in orders take 5-7 business days to be delivered. Books can be purchased by credit card at 1-800-986-0000 or on our website at www.legitstylespublishing.com. Incarcerated readers receive 25% discount. Please pay $11.25 and apply the same shipping terms as stated above.

www.ingramcontent.com/pod-product-compliance
Lightning Source LLC
Chambersburg PA
CBHW031151270326
41931CB00006B/231

9780996625272